Stevia Sweet Recipes

Sugar-Free—Naturally!

Jeffrey Goettemoeller

Stevia Sweet Recipes: Sugar-Free—Naturally!
by Jeffrey Goettemoeller.

Copyright © 1998 Jeffrey Goettemoeller,
Second Edition, 1999.

All rights reserved.

No part of this book may be reproduced in any form without the written consent of the publisher.

Printed in the United States of America by United Graphics, Inc., Mattoon, IL on recycled paper using soy based ink.

Cover Design by Studio 2D, Champaign, IL.

Interior illustrations by Susan Cavaciuti.

Vital Health Publishing
P.O. Box 544
Bloomingdale, IL 60108

ISBN: 1-890612-13-8

Table of Contents:

Introduction

Most of us crave sweets. Food processors have learned to exploit this craving by adding highly refined sweeteners to processed foods. You don't have to subject yourself to all that unhealthy food! Stevia is a healthy, delicious alternative to sugars and artificial sweeteners. Delicious, that is, if you use a recipe designed for stevia.

A child's first candy bar could be the start of an addiction to sweets. Sugar makes us feel "good," but only for a while. Sweets can become "comfort" foods and that's when we're hooked. There are many fine books which explain the details of why refined sugars and other sweeteners are harmful. Suffice it to say, there is more to these health problems than tooth decay and weight gain. There are serious concerns with artificial sweeteners as well. I encourage you to look into the subject before you choose to consume foods loaded with refined sugar or artificial sweeteners.

Years ago, I gave up refined sugars and honey to see if I could break the addiction cycle. I didn't know about stevia yet, and it was difficult at first, but soon I was happier and healthier without sugar. I can tell you from my own experience that stevia, even though many times sweeter than sugar, does not produce mood swings, hyperactivity, and addiction as does sugar.

When I stopped eating sugar, I discovered how tightly desserts are woven into our social structure. At first, I felt practically un-American, refusing a piece of apple pie after a supper. A young man like me is supposed to eat his dessert! I became accustomed to surprised reactions at my abstaining from sweets, but my mother proceeded do something about the situation.

My mother, who loves to cook for her children, knows I won't eat artificial sweeteners such as saccharin or aspartame, and she won't eat them either. One day we were shopping at *A to Z's Fresh Air Fair* health food store in Saint Joseph, Missouri and I heard Mom ask for stevia, a natural alternative to those artificial sweeteners. So began our multi-faceted adventure with this amazing herb.

My desire is that this book will help you kick the sugar habit and feel better as a result. Stevia tickles the taste buds as sugar does, but the resemblance stops there. Stevia has been shown to have beneficial medicinal effects. In fact, stevia may be sold in the United States only as a dietary supplement. Under today's FDA regulations, the sweetness is considered a "side effect." This is why stevia is not currently used in processed products here in the United States. This means we must cook with stevia for ourselves in order to make full use of this very fortunate "side effect."

Happy Cooking !

A Message from the Cook

Food preparation has always been a joy for me from the days I first stood on a chair to reach the table top. I had a fine teacher, my mother. Being farmers, most of our foods were fresh and unaltered. Our family enjoyed some delicious meals.

Home economics classes in high school and college broadened my views and presented new concepts in handling foods. I became acutely aware of the link between wholesome foods and family health. During the 1940's and 1950's giant food production industries emerged together with the need for processing to lengthen shelf life. Farmers were urged to use chemicals for pest control. Environmental conditions for food production worsened.

As a graduate home economist and then wife and mother, my interest in foods continued. In a kitchen feeding a family of eight, lots of planning, buying, storing, cooking, serving, and of course, cleanup went on. So did visits to doctors, hospitals, health food stores, nutrition lectures, libraries, book stores, and short courses. I wanted to improve my family's health and provide appealing, nutritious meals. Changing recipes to include more wholesome ingredients has been an ongoing, enjoyable challenge.

People tend to have a psychological attachment to the daily foods or dishes served them in childhood and adolescence. Desserts have been an important part of midwest family meals during my lifetime. Judging from 19th century cookbooks, our ancestors liked them too. Human beings do seem to have a "sweet tooth," a natural condition shared by all in varying degrees. A problem arises when liberal amounts of refined sugars are consumed on a steady basis. I would encourage you to read *Sugar Blues* by William Dufty, for more information.

Several years ago I heard of stevia, an herbal sweetener now used in many parts of the world. My family and I started using it in traditional dessert recipes. We were pleased with the results and really amazed at "how sweet it is!" In 1997 My son, Jeffrey, began a study of stevia as an alternative agricultural crop. We already had a collection of recipes using stevia. Producing a book was the next step. Jeffrey researched the sweet subject and entered the data into his computer.

These *Stevia Sweet Recipes* are here for your use and pleasure. Enjoy preparing, and especially eating them. Good health and God's blessing to you.

Bertha Goettemoeller

Acknowledgments

I am pleased to thank my mother, Bertha Goettemoeller, who made this book possible by developing most of the recipes and nurturing me in so many ways all my life. I also want to thank three other recipe contributors. They are my sister, Rosanna Goettemoeller, my niece, Elizabeth Cole, and Steve Marsden of *Herbal Advantage, Inc.*

Thanks to all the taste testers. They also played an important role. These include the Cole family; Pat, Yvonne (my sister), Jerome, Daniel, Benjamin, Elizabeth, Joseph, Rebecca, and Joshua (my nieces and nephews). My other siblings helped out as well: Dareth, Rosanna, Karen, and Adrian. There were many others with whom I had the pleasure of sitting around the kitchen table, enjoying tasty food and pleasant conversation.

A heartfelt thank you to Alex Ching, Ph.D. for allowing me to participate his stevia cultivation research. I appreciate his desire to teach and his friendship.

Finally, I want to thank David Richard, my editor at *Vital Health Publishing*. He played an important role in shaping this recipe book. I value his advice and guidance.

Chapter 1
All About Stevia

Stevia rebaudiana is an inconspicuous herb native to sections of Paraguay and Brazil in the subtropical part of South America. The plant resembles mint, but reaches 2-3 feet in height and does not spread so readily. The stems take root easily and form new plants, but propagation from seed is more difficult because of low germination rates.

Native Guarani Indians used stevia for centuries before M.S. Bertoni "discovered" it in 1887[2]. Outsiders had some catching up to do, but soon stevia was being scrutinized with that new-world mainstay, the scientific research study.

In my opinion, stevia is one of the great botanical discoveries of all time. In the United States, the potential for stevia has not yet been fully realized as it has in other countries.

Research Review

How sweet is it?

Green stevia powder and dried stevia leaves are up to 15 times sweeter than cane sugar[2]. Stevia extract powder may be up to 300 times sweeter than sugar[2]. This means it takes very little to sweeten a recipe, so cost must be evaluated on that basis.

Safety

Stevia has undergone numerous toxicity tests. None of these tests have shown any harmful effects[1]. Few substances can make this claim. The real test, though, was centuries of continuous use by natives of South America[1]. In addition, thousands of tons of stevia extracts have been consumed over the last 20 years in many countries with no harmful effects reported.[2]

Calories

Because of the unique structure of the glycoside molecules, the number of calories we get from stevia is almost zero[2]. Some of the recipes are high in calories due to other ingredients, so do be careful about recipe selection if you are trying to limit calories in your diet.

Regulating Blood Sugar

Stevia has been long been "prescribed" by herbalists in Brazil[2]. Stevia is thought to have a regulating effect on blood sugar levels[2]. These effects have not been confirmed. More research is certainly warranted in this area.

Cardiovascular Effect

The long term use of stevia is thought to produce mild strengthening of the heart and vascular system[2]. Here again, more research is needed.

Anti-Cavity Effect

Research has shown that many strains of harmful bacteria do not thrive in the presence of stevioside[2]. This has led to the use of stevia in products such as mouthwash and toothpaste. Unlike sugar, stevia may actually be good for your teeth. What a switch!

Digestive Aid Action

While this action has not been proven, stevia has been used in Brazil as an aid to digestive functioning[1].

Sources For this Chapter

1. Elkins, Rita (1997) *Stevia: Nature's Sweetener.* Pleasant Grove UT: Woodland Publishing

2. Richard, David (1996) *Stevia Rebaudiana: Nature's Sweet Secret.* Bloomingdale IL: Vital Health Publishing

Additional Recommended Reading

Healthy Habits
Authors: David and Anne Frahm
Publisher: Pinon Press

How to Grow Stevia
Author: Blas Oddone
Publisher: Guarani Botanicals

Stevia Miracle of No Calorie
Author: Donna Coates
Publisher: Random House Value Publishing

A search of the Worldwide Web on the Internet is a good way to learn more about stevia.

Chapter 2

Cooking with Stevia

This chapter explains the special factors we had to consider when developing recipes. If you want to experiment with your own recipes or understand ours better, this information will help. We also include general cooking tips and a valuable list of substitutions and measurements.

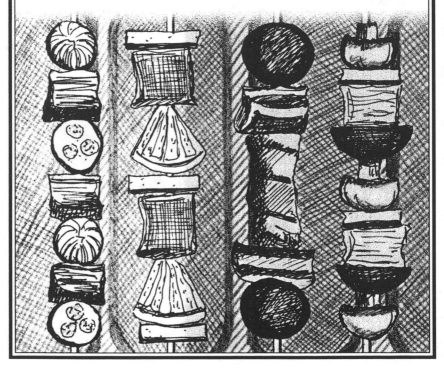

Stevia Products Used in the Recipes

If you can't find what you want, ask your local natural food store to order it for you. There are multiple wholesale sources for these forms of stevia. Hopefully grocery stores will soon begin to stock them as well.

I recommend using the Dried Stevia Leaves (for tea) or Green Stevia Powder whenever possible, just as I would recommend whole wheat over white flour. These forms provide the full range of nutrients found in stevia plants. For recipes that do not work well with Green Stevia Powder, however, I feel that Stevia Extract Powder is certainly preferable to sugar or artificial sweeteners. Liquid extracts of stevia are available, but we prefer the powders. Following is an overview of the stevia forms used in this book.

Dried Stevia Leaves

These whole, dried leaves of the stevia plant contain 8-12% sweet glycosides and work well for tea. You can purchase leaves or harvest from homegrown stevia plants. Simply pick the leaves before blossoming and dry on screens or in a food dehydrator on low heat.

Green Stevia Powder

We list this as an option in recipes that lend themselves to its use. In other recipes, this form doesn't work as well. It is a fine, green powder made from dried leaves and green stems of the Stevia plant. No other processing is done. Green Stevia Powder will impart varying shades of green to some recipes, depending on the amount used. This is the least refined product you can use in non-beverage recipes.

Stevia Extract Powder, 85-95% Sweet Glycosides

This is the primary stevia product used in the recipes. Sweet glycosides are extracted through one of several processes, usually water or ethyl alcohol based. The resulting fine, fluffy powder is 200-250 times sweeter than cane sugar and usually off-white. Any extract with glycosides in the range of 85-95% will work in our recipes, and this is the most common type on the market. If you should happen to find a product with a lower glycoside proportion, adjust the amount used accordingly.

I consider any stevia extract far superior to artificial sweeteners or sugar, but I do recommend using one that has not been artificially "bleached." Unfortunately, it is not always easy to determine if a given product contains bleach.

Cooking Tips

Stevia cannot simply be inserted where a recipe says "sugar." Several factors must be considered. Study the following information and you will be prepared to use this sweet herb in your cooking. The guidelines assume that stevia is replacing sugar.

Flavor Enhancement

Green Stevia Powder can enhance flavors in some dishes when used in small amounts, while it may not work at all in others. Our recipes are carefully designed to take advantage of this and other aspects of stevia.

Amount of Stevia

By volume, much less stevia than sugar is required. For sweetening purposes, approximately one teaspoon Stevia Extract Powder or three to four teaspoons Green Stevia Powder is used instead of one cup of sugar.

Sugarfree

In this book, "sugarfree" ingredients refers to those with no refined sugar.

Storing Stevia

Stevia keeps quite well, so go ahead and buy it in bulk if you wish. A sealed jar or plastic container is best for long term storage. Do not refrigerate.

Browning Qualities

Some stevia recipes brown less than similar dishes utilizing sugar or honey. Browning can be improved using other ingredients such as fats or milk.

Dry-Liquid Ingredient ratio

For baking with stevia, use either slightly less liquid or slightly more flour than would be used in recipes with sugar.

Mixing

Stevia is much fluffier than sugar. It scatters with the slightest disturbance. Recipe directions call for thoroughly mixing stevia with either dry or liquid ingredients. For sweetening raw fruits, first dissolve stevia in a teaspoon or two of lemon juice or water and then stir into the fruit.

Bakeware

Use stainless steel or oven-proof glassware if the food is to be left in the pan after baking.

Preheating the Oven

Observe the time your oven takes to preheat. Turn it on at the appropriate time while mixing ingredients.

About Flour

Whole grain flours will give the most for your money both in flavor and nutrition, but do be careful in storing them. Refrigerate if you plan to use in a few days. Otherwise, whole grain flours should be kept in the freezer. All of the following flours are whole grain except for the Unbleached White Flour.

Sifting

Do not sift flour before measuring. Just spoon flour into the measuring cup and level with the flat edge of a knife.

Varieties of Flour

Whole Wheat Flour

Quite versatile, this flour is usually ground from the so-called "hard" wheat berry. All wheat flours are rich in gluten, the substance that holds bread together.

Whole Wheat Pastry Flour

This one is produced by grinding "soft" wheat. It is ideal for desserts and general baking, substituting well for unbleached white flour.

Unbleached White Flour

The germ has been removed from the wheat berry to make this flour, but it does not undergo the bleaching process and it will store without refrigeration or freezing.

Barley Flour

Almost white in color, Barley Flour has a nutty flavor and a bit of gluten.

Rice Flour

In baked products, this flour gives a slightly grainy texture and a nice flavor. It is light in color and gluten-free.

Rye Flour

This flour has little gluten, but combines well with wheat flour for breads.

Oat Flour

Used in desserts and main dishes, Oat Flour contains very little gluten. It is available at some specialty stores or you can make your own from rolled oats. For one cup oat flour, measure out a cup and one tablespoon rolled oats and grind briefly in a blender or food processor.

Other Ingredients

Agar Agar
Made from seaweed, this vegetable gel serves as a vegetarian substitute for animal derived gelatin. It has been used for centuries to thicken various dishes.

Almonds, blanched
Add almonds to a saucepan with one inch of boiling water. Cover the pan, turn off heat and leave for 30 to 45 seconds. Drain and slip skins off nuts.

Almond Meal
For 1 1/4 cups meal process 1 cup raw almonds in a blender bowl. This requires only a few seconds. Store in a freezer or refrigerator.

Arrowroot Powder
This starch comes from a tuberous root and looks like cornstarch. It is used in the same way, making it a good choice for those allergic to corn.

Bananas, frozen
Buy medium ripe fruit. Break peeled bananas in half, place in freezer bags, and freeze. These frozen bananas slice easily for recipes or use the chunks as directed.

Carob Powder
This sweet brown powder looks like cocoa and some say there is a flavor resemblance. It contains no caffeine.

Coconut Meal

For one-half cup coconut meal, place one cup of unsulphured flaked coconut in a food processor or blender bowl. Process for a few seconds to the desired texture.

Cream Cheese

Choose cream cheese with the fat content you need. Neufchatel cheese can substitute for low fat cream cheese. Be sure to read labels.

Flavorings

Slightly more vanilla extract is needed when using stevia. Personal taste varies widely, so experiment and use the amount that tastes best to you.

Margarine

Non-hydrogenated margarine is a good alternative to butter. It usually contains canola or soy oil. Look for it at health food stores.

Nuts or Coconut, Toasting

Place nuts or coconut in a shallow baking pan and spread to the edges. Cook for five to ten minutes in a 350 degree oven.

Rice Beverage

This beverage comes in a carton and can replace dairy milk in many recipes.

Salt

If preferred, salt can be omitted from most recipes. The flavor will be slightly different in some cases. Also remember that unsalted butter is available.

Soy Beverage

This liquid product is found in many grocery stores, packaged in cartons on non-refrigerated shelves.

Soy Beverage Powder
Look in a health food store or some grocery stores for this powder.

Substitutions and Measurements

- 2 tablespoons butter = 1 ounce
- 1 stick or 1/4 pound butter = 1/2 cup
- 1 cup butter = 7/8 cup oil
- 1 cup buttermilk = 3/4 cup plain low fat yogurt plus 1/4 cup milk
- 1 cup sour cream = 7/8 cup plain yogurt
- 1 medium apple = 1 cup chopped apple
- 1 pound apples = 3 cups sliced apples
- 1 pound whole dates = 1 3/4 cups chopped dates
- 1 pound raisins = 2 3/8 cups raisins
- 1 whole orange = 6 to 8 tablespoons juice
- 1 medium to large lemon = 1/4 cup juice
- 5 1/3 ounces nutmeats = 1 cup chopped nutmeats
- 1 pound walnuts in shell = 2 cups shelled walnuts
- 1 pound almonds in shell = 1 cup shelled almonds
- ¼ pound chopped walnuts = about 1 cup
- 1 tablespoon cornstarch for cooking = 2 tablespoons flour
- 1 tablespoon arrowroot powder for thickening = 2 tablespoons flour
- 1 teaspoon baking powder = 1/4 teaspoon baking soda plus 1/2 teaspoon cream of tartar
- 3 ounce package flavored gelatin = 1 envelope unflavored gelatin + 2 cups fruit juice
- 3 teaspoons = 1 tablespoon
- 4 tablespoons = 1/4 cup
- About 5 1/2 tablespoons = 1/3 cup
- 1 cup = 8 fluid ounces
- 2 cups = 1 pint
- 4 cups = 1 quart

Chapter 3
Satisfying Breakfasts

Juicy, fresh fruits make a delightful breakfast, require very little preparation, and really please the palate. For fruits needing a bit of sweetening, it's easy to dissolve stevia in water or lemon juice and stir with the fruit pieces.

Wheat is intentionally omitted from the pancake recipe, a plus for those wishing to avoid it. Barley and rye flours make these pancakes big on whole grain goodness. Pour on some Maple Apple Syrup and begin your day with a smile!

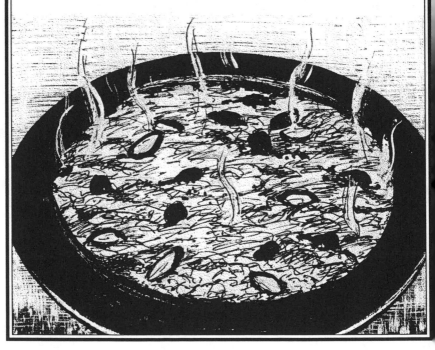

Golden Nectar Breakfast Shakes Yields 2 servings

Enjoy Breakfast with this creamy blend of favorite fruits.

- 2 bananas, broken in half
- 1/16 teaspoon Stevia Extract Powder
- 1/2 cup orange juice
- 1 1/2 cups unsweetened fresh or frozen peach slices
- Banana slices and mint sprigs for garnish, optional

Using a blender, process bananas, stevia, and orange juice. Add peach slices one at a time and process until smooth.

Pour into tall glasses and garnish, if desired.

Variation: For added fiber, blend in 1 tablespoon oat bran with the bananas. Increase juice to 2/3 cup.

Wheat Free Barley-Rye Pancakes
Yields 12 large pancakes

Quick and Easy to fix and memorable to eat!

- 1/4 teaspoon Stevia Extract Powder
- 1 1/2 cups barley flour
- 1/2 cup rye flour
- 3 teaspoons baking powder
- 1/2 teaspoon cream of tartar
- 1/4 teaspoon salt
- 2 eggs
- 2 tablespoons vegetable oil
- 1/2 cup soymilk or vanilla flavored soy beverage
- 1 1/4 cups water

Stir together dry ingredients. In a separate bowl mix all liquids and then combine the two mixtures.

Heat the griddle. Ladle about 1/3 cup pancake batter onto the griddle for each pancake. Turn when bubbly on top and underside is browned.

Serve hot with Maple Apple Syrup, Pineapple Sauce, or Spicy Applesauce (see index).

Variations:
- Use 1 cup soymilk and decrease water to 3/4 cup.
- Decrease salt to 1/8 teaspoon.
- Substitute oat flour for rye flour

Maple Apple Syrup Yields 1 1/4 cups

Serve hot over pancakes or waffles

- 1/4 cup water
- 1 cup natural apple juice
- 1 tablespoon arrowroot or cornstarch
- 1 tablespoon butter, optional
- 1/4 teaspoon Stevia Extract Powder
- 3/4 teaspoon vanilla flavoring
- 3/4 teaspoon maple flavoring

Stir together water, apple juice, and arrowroot powder. Bring to a boil over medium heat. Reduce heat to simmer and cook an additional 2 minutes. Remove from heat and stir in remaining ingredients. Refrigerate leftovers in a covered jar.

Breakfast Fruit Bowl Yields 1 or 2 servings

Juicy, sweet fruit with Crunchy Granola.

- 1 pear
- 1 apple
- 1 teaspoon fresh lemon juice
- 1/16 teaspoon Stevia Extract Powder
- 2 or 3 teaspoons water
- 1/4 to 1/2 cup Crunchy Granola (see index)
- plain, unsweetened yogurt (optional)

Peel, core, and cube the pear and apple. Place in a bowl. In a cup, mix lemon juice, stevia, and 1 teaspoon water. Stir the lemon juice mixture into the fruit. Rinse cup with the remaining 2 teaspoons of water and add this to fruit mixture. Spoon granola over the fruit. If desired, top with yogurt.

Variation: Try using other fruit such as banana, kiwi, or grapes.

Crunchy Granola

Yields 6 cups

A spiced, drier version of granola.

- 3/4 cup oat bran
- 2 1/2 cups rolled oats
- 1/2 cup unsulphured coconut meal
- 1/2 cup almond meal
- 1/4 cup sesame seeds
- 1/2 cup unsweetened applesauce
- 3/4 teaspoon Stevia Extract Powder OR 2 teaspoons Green Stevia Powder
- 1 1/2 teaspoons cinnamon
- dash each of cloves and nutmeg
- 1/3 cup vegetable oil
- 1/2 to 3/4 cup raisins (optional)

In a large mixing bowl, stir together bran, rolled oats, coconut meal, almond meal, and sesame seeds. Set aside.

Combine applesauce, stevia, spices, and oil in a small bowl. Add to the oat mixture and stir. Turn onto a lightly oiled 10 x 15 x 1 inch baking pan. Bake for 20 minutes in a 300 degree preheated oven. Remove from the oven and stir. Bake an additional 15 minutes. Granola will be golden brown.

Cool the pan on a rack. Stir in raisins, if used. Spoon into a storage container and cover. Leave at room temperature overnight. Refrigerate or freeze.

Almond and Fruit Granola

Yields 6 cups

Like eating little chunks of cookies.

- 2 cups rolled oats
- 1 cup unsulphured coconut meal
- 1/2 cup coarse almond meal
- 1/4 cup sesame seeds
- 1 cup unsweetened applesauce
- 3/4 teaspoon Stevia Extract Powder
- 1/4 cup vegetable oil
- 1/2 teaspoon vanilla extract
- 1/2 cup chopped dates
- 1/2 cup raisins
- 1/2 cup chopped almonds

In a large bowl stir together oats, coconut, almond meal, and sesame seeds. Set aside.

Stir together applesauce, stevia, oil, and vanilla extract. Add to the oat mixture and blend well to a clumpy texture. Set aside 20 minutes so the oats can absorb moisture. Spread on a lightly oiled 10 x 15 x 1 inch pan. Bake for 20 minutes in a 300 degree preheated oven. Remove from oven and stir. Return to the oven for an additional 15 minutes of baking. The granola will be lightly browned. Cool the pan on a wire rack.

Add fruit and chopped almonds to the granola mixture and stir. Spoon into a storage container and cover. Leave at room temperature overnight. For storage longer than one week, freeze.

27

Sunday Best Oatmeal

Yields 2 or 3 servings

Start the day with this nutritious hot cereal and tasty toppings.

- 1 3/4 cup water
- 1/16 teaspoon salt (optional)
- 1/3 to 1/2 teaspoon Stevia Extract Powder
- 1 cup old fashioned rolled oats

Toppings:
- milk or yogurt
- chopped pecans
- raisins
- coconut
- cinnamon

Place water, salt, and stevia in a medium saucepan. Bring to a boil and stir in oats. Reduce heat to medium and cook an additional 5 minutes. Stir as needed.

Remove from heat, cover, and leave 3 or 4 minutes. Spoon into cereal bowls and add any of the above toppings.

Variation: For added fiber, replace 1 1/2 tablespoons of the rolled oats with 1 tablespoon oat bran. Cook as above.

Chapter 4

Refreshing Beverages

The following taste tempting beverages not only add pleasure to life, but are kind to your body as well.

A pot of herbal tea can warm the heart and please the soul. Herbal coffee substitutes offer their own rich flavors and aromas. Keep a pitcher of cold mint tea in the refrigerator for quenching summertime thirst or make a tangy-sweet lemonade any time of the year. Start with only a pinch of stevia to sweeten a cup of tea.

Banana Kiwi Blend

- 2 frozen bananas
- 2 kiwi fruit, peeled
- 1 pear, peeled, cored, and quartered
- 1 cup cooked, crushed pineapple
- ⅛ teaspoon Green Stevia Powder
- 2 tablespoons soy or rice beverage powder
- ½ cup apple juice

Prepare bananas the previous day. Peel, halve, and drop into a plastic bag. Freeze.

Place remaining ingredients in the blender bowl in the order given. Process on high to mix thoroughly. Add banana pieces, one at a time, and blend until smooth. Serve.

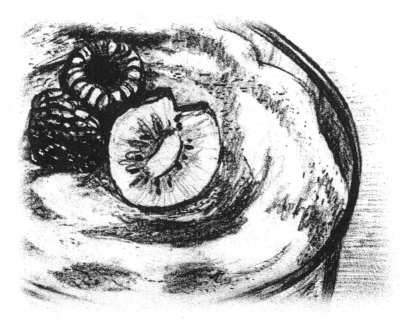

Almond Milk

Unblanched almonds may also be used in this recipe.

- 2 cups cold water
- 1/2 cup almonds, blanched (see index)
- 1/8 to 1/4 teaspoon Stevia Extract Powder
- 1/4 teaspoon vanilla extract

Using 1/2 cup of the water, soak almonds 1 to 2 hours. Do not drain. Pour into the blender bowl and process on high about 1 minute. Add remaining water, stevia, and vanilla extract. Blend to form a smooth milk. Strain through a fine sieve, if you wish. Reserve pulp for another use. Cover and refrigerate milk and pulp.

Shake before using as separation occurs naturally. Best if used within a day, but may be kept 2 days.

Tip: If the milk is to be used for a "smoothie," there is no need to strain out pulp.

Pear Berry Shake

A nutritious, satisfying treat with refreshing flavor.

- 1/2 cup water
- 1 fresh pear; cored, pared, and quartered
- 2 tablespoons soy or rice beverage powder
- 1/4 teaspoon vanilla extract
- 1/8 teaspoon Stevia Extract Powder
- 1 or 2 teaspoons fresh lemon juice
- 1 1/4 cups frozen strawberries

Place all ingredients, except strawberries, in a blender bowl. Process briefly to cut up pears. Gradually add strawberries and continue processing to produce a smooth beverage. Serve.

Variation: Use 3/4 cup frozen blueberries in place of strawberries.

Cherry Vanilla Shake

Yields 3 servings

Enjoy this cold and smooth "dessert in a glass."

- 2 bananas, frozen
- 1/2 cup yogurt OR soy yogurt
- 2 tablespoons nonfat dry milk OR rice beverage powder
- 1/4 teaspoon Stevia Extract Powder
- 1 teaspoon vanilla extract
- 2/3 cup white grape juice
- 1 1/2 cups red tart cherries, fresh or frozen

Prepare bananas the day before serving. Peel, halve and drop in a plastic bag. Freeze.

Place remaining ingredients in blender bowl and process to mix. Add banana halves, one at a time, and process until smooth.

Strawberry Smoothie

Yields 2 servings

A delicious way to include more fruit in your diet.

- 1 large banana
- 2/3 cup natural white grape juice
- 1/16 teaspoon Stevia Extract Powder
- 3 tablespoons tofu OR plain yogurt
- 2 tablespoons nonfat dry milk, optional
- 2 cups frozen strawberries

Place all ingredients, except strawberries, in the blender bowl and process to mix. Add strawberries gradually and process until smooth. Serve.

Tip: Make this smoothie with <u>fresh</u> strawberries by using a <u>frozen</u> banana.

Peanut Butter Milk Shake

Yields 2 servings

Thick, rich, and creamy.

- 2 frozen bananas
- 1 cup natural apple juice
- 1/2 cup water
- 3 or 4 tablespoons natural peanut butter
- 1/4 teaspoons Stevia Extract Powder
- 1 teaspoon vanilla extract
- 1 cup nonfat dry milk OR 1/2 cup soy beverage powder

    Prepare bananas a day in advance. Peel, halve and drop in a freezer bag. Freeze.

    Measure the next 6 ingredients into a blender bowl. Process to mix, then add the banana pieces one at a time. Blend until smooth. Serve.

Variation: Any nut butter may be used.

Yerba Mate Tea

Yields 4 (6 ounce) servings

The traditional stevia sweetened beverage of South America!

- Boiling water
- 1 tablespoon yerba matte leaves
- 3 cups freshly boiled water
- few drops lemon juice, optional
- 1/4 teaspoon Green Stevia Powder

Warm a teapot by rinsing with boiling water. Place tea leaves into a tea ball and set into warmed teapot. Add freshly boiled water and allow to steep for 5 to 10 minutes. Remove tea ball and stir in stevia. Add lemon juice if used. Serve.

Iced Stevia Mint Tea

Yields five (6 ounce) servings

A cold, refreshing taste sensation.

- 4 cups water
- 4 tablespoons Dried Stevia Leaves (pack leaves into the measuring cup)
- 2 tablespoons dry mint leaves, crushed.
- Ice

Bring 2 cups water to a boil, stir in stevia and mint leaves. Turn off heat and allow tea to steep 5 to 8 minutes. Strain into a 2 quart glass jar.

Cool tea to room temperature and add remaining water. Pour over ice and serve.

Variation: One teaspoon of freshly squeezed lemon juice can be added to the tea.

Hot Stevia Ginger Tea

A unique blend of sweet and spicy in a refreshing tea.

- Boiling water
- 1 1/2 tablespoons Dried Stevia Leaves
- 1 tablespoon dry mint leaves
- 3 cups freshly boiled water
- 2 teaspoons Ginger Tea Concentrate (see index)

The teapot should be warmed by rinsing it with boiling water.

Measure the Stevia and mint leaves into a tea ball. Place the tea ball in the warmed pot and add the 3 cups of freshly boiled water. Allow to steep 5 minutes.

Remove the tea ball and stir in the Ginger Tea Concentrate. Serve.

Variation: Add a squeeze of lemon juice.

Tip: Lightly crush the dry leaves as you fill the tea ball to release more flavor.

Hot & Mellow Herbal Beverage   Yields 1 cup

An all-natural beverage the entire family can enjoy.

- Freshly boiled water
- Instant herbal beverage powder*
- Stevia Extract Powder or Green Stevia Powder

Pour water into a coffee cup. Stir in one teaspoon beverage powder and stevia to taste. Begin with just a pinch of stevia.

Variations:
- Stir in a sprinkle of ground cinnamon. Add nonfat dry milk to taste or soy beverage powder.
- Use 2 teaspoons herbal beverage powder and pour over ice for a refreshing cold drink.
- Add finely grated orange peel.

*Tip: Instant herbal beverage powders contain roasted cereals such as rye and barley, and herbs such as chicory. Some resemble coffee in flavor, but contain no caffeine. Herbal beverage powder is available at your local health food store and most grocery stores.

Marsden's Spiced Coffee
Yields 8 cups of coffee

A spicy sweet coffee treat.

- 6 cups cold water
- 3 to 5 tablespoons decaffeinated ground coffee
- 1 to 3 teaspoons Green Stevia Powder
- 1 tablespoon Cinnamon Spice Tea Mix

Follow manufacturer's instructions for your coffee maker.

Pour in water. Line coffee basket with a filter and add the coffee. Make a depression in coffee for the stevia and top both with the Tea Mix. Turn on heat. After cycle finishes, serve coffee hot.

Variations:
- Add your favorite dairy or non-dairy creamers.
- For an elegant dessert coffee, add a dollop of Whipped Cream (see index) and finely shredded orange peel.

Tip: Cinnamon Spice Tea Mix is available at grocery or health food stores.

Cherry Lime Cooler
Yields six (6 ounce) servings

Raspberry also combines well with lime.

- 2 1/2 cups water
- 1/8 teaspoon Stevia Extract Powder
- 3 tablespoons fresh lime juice
- 2 cups sugar free cherry juice blend (available in health food stores or frozen in grocery stores)

Place all ingredients in a 2 quart glass jar and shake to dissolve the stevia. Store, covered, in the refrigerator. Serve chilled.

Ginger Tea Concentrate

Yields 3/4 cup

Adds zing to beverages, main dishes, and fruit desserts.

- 3 inch piece of raw gingerroot
- 1 cup water
- 2 teaspoons Stevia Extract Powder

Wrap and freeze the remaining raw gingerroot for later use. DO NOT use ground ginger in this recipe.

Peel and thinly slice gingerroot and simmer in water for 30 minutes. Strain liquid into a pint jar. There will be about 3/4 cup of concentrate. Add stevia and stir to dissolve. Cover and refrigerate.

For a cup of ginger tea, stir 1/2 to 1 teaspoon Concentrate into a cup of hot water. A pinch of Stevia Extract Powder or Green Stevia Powder can be used for a sweeter tea.

Fresh Lemonade

Yields 2 quarts

The finest of summer beverages.

- 3/4 cup fresh lemon juice (juice from about 3 lemons)
- 1 teaspoon Stevia Extract Powder
- 7 1/4 cups water

Place the lemon juice and stevia in a 2 quart glass jar. Shake briefly to dissolve the stevia.

Add water and stir. Cover and refrigerate. This beverage is usually served chilled. It is also delicious at room temperature.

Adjust the amount of lemon juice and stevia as desired. Variations:

- To serve over ice, reduce the water to 6 cups.
- For a hint of ginger, stir in 1 1/2 teaspoons Ginger Tea Concentrate (see index).

Chapter 5

Hearty Baked Breads

The enticing aroma of baking bread always brings compliments as guests arrive. Family and friends will want 'seconds' when you serve these whole grain muffins, buns, coffee cakes and loaves of bread.

Stevia combines well with the other ingredients and sweetens delightfully. Adjust the amount of stevia as you like.

For a tender crust, rub oil or butter on the bread as it comes from the oven, or leave "as is" for a crisp crust. Most breads will freeze well. Just be sure to use an air-tight wrap. Thaw on a rack at room temperature.

Oatmeal Banana Bread

Yields 1 loaf

A fruity, whole grain quick bread.

- 2 1/3 cups whole wheat pastry flour
- 3/4 teaspoon Stevia Extract Powder
- 2 1/2 teaspoons baking powder
- 1/4 teaspoon baking soda
- 1/4 teaspoon salt, optional
- 1 cup rolled oats
- 1/4 cup currants
- 1/2 cup chopped dates
- 3/4 cup water
- 1 cup mashed bananas (about 3)
- 1/2 cup vegetable oil
- 2 eggs
- 2 teaspoons vanilla extract

Butter and flour a 9 x 5 inch bread pan.

Stir together flour, stevia, baking powder, soda, and salt. Add oats, currants, and dates, then stir briefly. Set aside.

In a medium bowl mix water, bananas, oil, eggs, and vanilla. Add the flour mixture and stir just to combine. Turn into prepared loaf pan. Bake at 350 degrees in a preheated oven for 55 to 60 minutes. Cool a few minutes in pan then remove to a rack.

Variation: Add 1/2 teaspoon cinnamon and 1/4 teaspoon nutmeg.

Raisin Wheat Bread Yields 2 loaves

Sweet and spicy, this loaf is festive enough for holidays, yet simple enough to bake everyday.

- 1 1/3 cups water
- 2 cups raisins
- 5 cups whole wheat flour OR unbleached white flour
- 1 packet dry yeast
- 1/8 teaspoon Stevia Extract Powder OR 3/8 teaspoon Green Stevia Powder
- 3 tablespoons butter, softened
- 1/2 teaspoon salt
- 1/2 teaspoon cinnamon
- 2 eggs

Bring raisins and water to a boil in a small saucepan. Turn off heat, cover pan and leave for 5 minutes. Drain, reserving liquid. Add water to measure 1 1/3 cups and pour into a large bowl. Cool to lukewarm.

Sprinkle yeast over liquid and allow to dissolve. Add 2 cups flour, stevia, butter, salt, cinnamon, and eggs. Beat briefly on low speed, scraping bowl as needed. Then beat on high 4 minutes. With a mixing spoon, work in raisins and as much flour as possible. Knead in enough of the remaining flour to make a stiff dough. Form dough into a ball and place in an oiled bowl. Oil top of dough, cover and set aside in a warm area for about an hour to double.

Punch down dough, form 2 long (12 inch) loaves and place on an oiled baking sheet. Cover and let rise to double size or about 30 minutes. Bake in a 375 degree preheated oven 20 to 25 minutes. Bread should sound hollow when tapped on the underside. Place on rack to cool.

Raspberry Cinnamon Rolls   Yields 12 large rolls

Feather-light dough with sweet, spicy filling.

- 1 teaspoon Stevia Extract Powder
- 1 tablespoon natural applesauce
- 1 cup plus 2 tablespoons warm water
- 1 packet dry yeast
- 1/3 cup vegetable oil
- 1 egg
- 1/4 to 3/4 teaspoon salt
- 2 cups whole wheat flour
- 1 1/3 cups unbleached white flour plus more for kneading
- 3 tablespoons butter, softened
- 1/2 cup sugarfree all-fruit raspberry spread
- cinnamon to taste
- 1/2 cup currants

Combine stevia, applesauce, and water in a medium bowl. Sprinkle in yeast and soften 10 minutes. Stir in oil, egg, salt, and whole wheat flour. Beat 3 minutes. Mix and knead in unbleached white flour, using more as needed to form soft dough. Oil bowl. Turn dough in bowl to oil top. Cover and chill 1 1/2 hours.

Punch down dough and roll on a floured surface to a 12 inch square. Use water to dampen a 1/2 inch strip along one side. Spread remaining surface with butter and raspberry spread. Sprinkle with cinnamon and currants. Start with edge opposite dampened edge and roll dough. Press dampened edge to seal. Cut into 12 pieces and place in an oiled 9 inch square baking pan. Cover and let rise in a warm place until double, about 40 minutes. Bake in a 400 degree preheated oven 15 to 18 minutes. Cool 5 minutes, turn out and serve hot.

Variation: For blueberry rolls, use 1 cup Blueberry Jam (see index) and omit currants.

Gourmet Wheat and Rye Bread   Yields 2 loaves

Hearty brown bread for dinner, sandwiches, or toasting.

- 1/2 cup rye flour
- 5 1/2 cups whole wheat flour
- 1/2 teaspoon Stevia Extract Powder
- 2 packets dry yeast
- 2 teaspoons salt
- 2 tablespoons natural apple juice
- 3 tablespoons butter
- 2 1/2 cups very hot water (not boiling)
- more wheat flour for kneading
- vegetable oil

In a large mixing bowl combine rye flour, 1 1/2 cups wheat flour, stevia, yeast, and salt. Stir well. Add juice and butter, then pour water over all. Stir well. Water should be just hot enough to melt most of the butter. Using an electric mixer on medium, beat for 2 minutes. Add 1 more cup of the flour and beat on high for 1 minute. Scrape down the sides of the bowl.

Using a wooden spoon, stir in enough of the remaining flour to form soft dough. Turn out on a floured surface and knead about 10 minutes or until smooth.

Cover dough with plastic wrap and set aside 15 minutes. Punch down and then form 2 loaves. Place in bread pans prepared with vegetable oil. Liberally oil the tops of the loaves. Cover with waxed paper. Place on a cookie sheet and cover all with a clean towel. Refrigerate 5 to 20 hours.

To bake, uncover and set aside 10 minutes. Place oven rack in a position about 1/3 of the way above the base. Bake loaves in a preheated oven at 350 degrees from 45 to 50 minutes. The bread is done when it sounds hollow if tapped on the underside. Place on a rack to cool.

Multi-Grain Dinner Rolls   Yields 3 to 4 dozen rolls

Tempting hot from the oven!

- 1 tablespoon natural apple juice
- 2 cups warm water
- 2 packets dry yeast
- 1/4 cup soft butter
- 1 cup rolled oats
- 1/2 cup cornmeal
- 1/2 cup wheat germ
- 1/2 teaspoon Stevia Extract Powder
- 1 1/2 teaspoon salt
- 2 eggs
- 4 to 6 cups unbleached white flour

Measure juice, water, and butter in a large bowl. Sprinkle on yeast and allow to soften 5 minutes. Meanwhile, process oatmeal and cornmeal in a blender until coarsely ground. Stir into yeast mixture along with wheat germ, 1 whole egg, 1 egg white, stevia, and salt. Reserve the egg yolk.

Gradually stir in the flour and then knead enough flour into the dough to make it easy to handle. Knead several minutes until smooth. Oil the top, cover bowl, and let rise in a warm place until doubled, about 1 hour.

Use oil or vegetable spray to prepare 1 large or 2 smaller pans. Form dough into rolls and place in pan. Sides of the rolls can be touching or not. Rolls placed further apart will cook faster. Let rise until almost doubled.

Preheat oven to 350 degrees. Mix egg yolk with 2 teaspoons water. Brush this on roll tops. This will help them to brown and be shiny. Discard any remaining yolk mixture. Bake to a light golden color or about 20 to 30 minutes. Baking time will depend on the size of the rolls and the space between them. Serve hot or allow to cool on racks.

Whole Wheat Burger Buns

Yields 24 buns

Perfect for your favorite veggie-burger or hamburger!

- 2 1/4 cups warm water
- 1/4 cup unsweetened applesauce
- 2 packets dry yeast
- 1 or 2 teaspoons salt
- 1 teaspoon Stevia Extract Powder
- 1/2 cup vegetable oil
- 2 eggs, lightly beaten
- 6 cups whole wheat flour

Place water and applesauce in a medium bowl. Sprinkle yeast into the mixture and leave to soften 5 minutes. Add salt, stevia, oil, and eggs. Stir well. Mix in the flour, stirring with a wooden spoon and then knead in the remainder, or as needed to form a medium dough. Oil the top of the dough, cover, and refrigerate about an hour.

Roll half the chilled dough to about 1/2 inch thickness in a rectangle measuring 9 x 12 inches. Using a 3 inch cutter, make 12 buns. Repeat with the remaining dough. Place buns on oiled cookie sheets in a warm location. Cover with a clean towel and allow to rise until doubled in bulk. Bake 10 minutes in a preheated 400 degree oven. Remove to racks and allow to cool. Store leftovers in an airtight container. Freezes well.

Strawberry Banana Muffins   Yields 12 muffins

Serve hot from the oven and be ready for compliments!

- 1 3/4 cups whole wheat pastry flour
- 3/8 teaspoon Stevia Extract Powder
- 2 1/2 teaspoons baking powder
- 1/2 teaspoon cinnamon
- 1 egg
- 1/2 cup water
- 1/4 cup vegetable oil
- 2/3 cup mashed banana (1 large banana)
- 3/4 cup chopped fresh strawberries

Oil the muffin cups. In a mixing bowl stir together flour, stevia, baking powder, and cinnamon. Make a depression to receive the liquid ingredients. Using a separate bowl, mix together egg, water, and oil. Add to the flour mixture and stir. Add banana and strawberries and stir just until combined.

Spoon batter into the muffin cups. Bake in a preheated oven at 400 degrees for 20 minutes or until golden.

Date Orange Coffee Cake

Yields 12 servings

This tender braided bread is filled with luscious fruit sauce.

- 1/4 cup raisins
- 1/2 cup chopped dates
- 1/4 teaspoon grated orange peel
- 1/2 cup orange juice
- 2 cups whole wheat pastry flour
- 1 tablespoon baking powder
- 1/8 teaspoon Stevia Extract Powder
- 1/4 teaspoon salt
- 1/3 cup butter
- 4 ounces regular or reduced fat cream cheese
- 1/2 cup milk or soymilk

In a small saucepan combine the first 4 ingredients and bring to a boil, stirring constantly. Reduce heat to low and cook until very thick, stirring as needed.

Remove from heat and cool to room temperature. Sift or stir together flour, baking powder, stevia, and salt. Cut in butter and cream cheese until crumbly. Add milk and stir just until mixed.

Tear a strip of waxed paper 20 inches long and sprinkle with flour. Place dough on the paper and sprinkle more flour on top. Pat or roll dough into an 8 x 12 inch rectangle. Invert dough onto an oiled baking sheet and remove paper.

Spread fruit filling down the center of the dough. Make 2 1/2 inch cuts from the long sides toward the center forming 1 inch wide strips. Fold strips atop filling alternating sides.

Bake in a preheated oven at 375 degrees for 20 to 25 minutes or until light golden. Best served warm but delicious cold also.

Chapter 6
Sensational Salads

Sensational salads are a part of healthy meals and they let your creativity blossom. There's a wide variety of foods which can go into salads and you get to make the choices.

Included in this chapter is a versatile recipe using agar agar to gel fruit juice.

Have you ever considered colorful blossoms as garnish? Make sure they're edible and remember tasty sprouts, herbs, and mushrooms as well. Celebrate with salads!

Summer Garden Coleslaw

Crunchy vegetables in a creamy yogurt dressing

- ½ cup chopped raw cauliflower
- 2 cups shredded cabbage
- ¾ cup shredded carrots
- ¼ cup pecans, toasted
- ⅓ cup currants
- ⅛ teaspoon Stevia Extract Powder
- 2 teaspoons fresh lemon juice
- few drops vanilla extract
- ½ cup plain yogurt or soy yogurt
- ginger powder (optional)

Use a large bowl to combine the first 5 ingredients.

For dressing, whisk together stevia, lemon juice, vanilla extract, and yogurt. Pour over the salad and toss briefly to combine.

Variation: Toasted, slivered almonds can replace pecans.

Apple Lentil Salad

Yields 5 Servings

Grow your own nutritious lentil sprouts!

- 2 cups chopped apples (2 apples) such as Braeburn or Jonathan
- 2 teaspoons fresh lemon juice
- 1/4 cup chopped walnuts
- 1/2 cup sprouted lentils
- 1/4 cup chopped celery
- 2 to 4 tablespoons currants
- 1/8 teaspoon Stevia Extract Powder
- 1/4 cup mayonnaise OR Basic Salad Dressing (see index)
- parsley sprigs for garnish, optional

Stir apples with lemon juice. Add walnuts, lentil sprouts, celery, and currants.

In a small bowl whisk stevia into mayonnaise. Spoon over salad and combine. Garnish and serve.

Tip: To sprout lentils, pour 1 cup water into a wide top pint jar and add 1/4 cup lentils from the grocery store. Secure nylon net over the top with a rubber band and leave on counter overnight. Next morning, pour off water. Tilt jar into a sauce dish in draining position. Cover. Rinse with tepid water 3 times a day. Use when sprouts are about 1/2 inch long. Refrigerate.

Ginger Banana Salad

Mellow fruit, spicy ginger, and crunchy almonds.

- Boston or Romaine lettuce leaves
- 2 slices cooked ginger from Ginger Tea Concentrate recipe (see index) or ground ginger to taste.
- 1/2 cup plain yogurt
- 1/8 teaspoon Stevia Extract Powder
- 4 bananas in 1/2 inch chunks
- 2 tablespoons slivered almonds
- 1 tablespoon unsulphured coconut
- Berries in season or lemon slices for garnish

Line a salad bowl with lettuce leaves.

Mince ginger. Mix with yogurt and stevia. Gently stir in bananas and almonds. Spoon into the prepared salad bowl and sprinkle with coconut, if used.

Garnish and serve.

Orange Sunrise Salad

An agar agar gelled salad packed with citrus flavor.

- 2 tablespoons agar agar
- 2½ cups orange juice
- ½ teaspoon grated lemon peel
- ½ teaspoon Stevia Extract Powder
- Salad greens
- Pecan halves
- Basic Salad Dressing (see index)

Place the first 4 ingredients in a medium saucepan. Stir and place over medium heat. Bring to a boil, reduce heat and simmer 5 minutes. Stir as needed.

Pour into a 6 x 10 inch dish. Chill to set, about 3 hours. Cut into 6 squares and place atop greens on salad plates. Spoon on some salad dressing and garnish with a pecan.

Country Potato Salad

Combine potatoes, eggs, and fresh herbs for this hearty salad.

- 2/3 cup Basic Salad Dressing (see index)
- 2 tablespoons minced, fresh parsley
- 1/2 teaspoon Garden Blend Seasoning (see index)
- 1/8 teaspoon Green Stevia Powder
- 1/2 teaspoon nutritional yeast flakes
- 1/4 teaspoon salt, or to taste
- 1 teaspoon Dijon-style mustard
- 2 tablespoons thinly sliced green onion.
- 4 tablespoons thinly sliced celery
- 2 tablespoons chopped green pepper
- 4 hard boiled eggs
- 4 medium potatoes, cooked and cubed (about 4 1/2 cups)
- 1 hard boiled egg and parsley sprigs for garnish

In a medium bowl mix salad dressing, parsley, Garden Blend Seasoning, stevia, yeast flakes, salt, mustard, and green onion. Fold in celery, green pepper, eggs, and potatoes.

Taste and adjust seasonings. Cover and chill.

Garnish and serve.

Vegetarian Gelled Fruit Salad   Yields 4 servings

An easy recipe for agar agar gelled salad.

- 2 cups unsweetened fruit juice (apple, white grape, cherry blends, orange, or others)
- 1/8 teaspoon Stevia Extract Powder
- 2 tablespoon agar agar
- a few drops of almond extract or other flavors compatible with the juice used
- lettuce leaves or alfalfa sprouts
- fruit pieces for garnish
- chopped nuts
- pour-on sauce such as those fruit sauces found in the "Sauces" chapter of this book

Be sure to measure accurately. Place juice, stevia, and agar agar in a small saucepan and mix well. Bring to a boil while stirring. Reduce heat and simmer 5 minutes to completely dissolve agar agar, stirring occasionally. Set aside for 15 minutes. Pour into molds or a bowl. Refrigerate, undisturbed, until firm.

To serve from the bowl, garnish with lettuce, alfalfa sprouts, fruit pieces, nuts, and sauce as desired. Molds should be dipped into hot water up to the brim, then loosened gently at the edges with the tip of a table knife. Unmold onto a bed of sprouts or lettuce, surrounded with pieces of fruit, and sprinkle with nuts. Serve with the desired sauce.

Herbed Tomato Slices

Yields 5 servings

Tomatoes marinated in a lightly sweetened sauce.

- 5 Roma tomatoes, sliced
- 1 tablespoon chopped fresh parsley
- 1 tablespoon chopped fresh basil leaves
- 2 tablespoons freshly squeezed lemon juice
- 1/16 teaspoon Stevia Extract Powder
- 1 tablespoon vegetable oil
- pinch of salt (optional)

Place tomatoes, parsley, and basil in a shallow casserole or serving bowl.

In a small jar, stir together the remaining ingredients. Pour over the tomatoes and cover with plastic wrap. Allow to marinate at room temperature 1 to 2 hours, stirring every 30 minutes. Serve!

Variation: Larger tomatoes can be used.

Carrot Pineapple Salad Mold   Yields 6 servings

A jazzy, gorgeous mold with a bit of crunch.

- 1 can (20 ounce) crushed pineapple OR 2 1/2 cups fresh pineapple chunks plus 1/2 cup water
- 1 packet unflavored gelatin
- 3/4 cup natural apple juice
- 1/4 teaspoon Stevia Extract Powder
- 1 tablespoon fresh lemon juice
- a few drops of almond extract
- 1 cup finely grated carrot (about 1 carrot)
- alfalfa sprouts, parsley, or leafy greens

Drain crushed pineapple. For fresh pineapple, simmer chunks in water 10 minutes. Drain, reserving liquid. Add water to the liquid, if necessary, to make 1 cup. Place liquid in a medium metal mixing bowl and sprinkle gelatin on top. Soften gelatin for 5 minutes and then dissolve over low heat.

Remove from heat and stir in apple juice, stevia, lemon juice, and almond extract. Add grated carrots and reserved pineapple pulp. Pour into a 1 quart mold. Chill several hours or overnight. To unmold, run the tip of a table knife around the upper edge to loosen salad. Invert on serving plate and place a hot cloth over the mold. Remove cloth and mold. Surround with sprouts, parsley, or greens.

Tip: Use either room temperature pineapple sauce or Garlic and Yogurt Salad Dressing (see index) to pour over the salad.

Mary's Mixed Green Salad

Best if prepared shortly before serving.

- 6 cups loosely packed torn, mixed greens (such as spinach, watercress, leaf lettuce, or Swiss chard)
- 1/2 cup thinly sliced sweet green peppers
- 1/2 cup broken pecan pieces, toasted if desired
- edible flowers* (optional)
- 1 recipe of Fresh Citrus Dressing OR Garlic and Yogurt Salad Dressing (see index).

Lightly toss together greens, green peppers, and pecans. Garnish with edible flowers, if used. Pass the salad dressing.

*Tip: Choose fresh, unsprayed blossoms such as nasturtium or violet, found in the produce section of food markets, or homegrown, making sure they are edible.

Nectarines and Berries

Luscious golden sauce covers mixed fruit.

- 4 fresh nectarines
- 1/8 teaspoon Stevia Extract Powder
- 2 teaspoons lemon juice, freshly squeezed
- 2 cups fresh or frozen mixed berries such as strawberries, blackberries, or raspberries
- sliced blanched almonds for garnish

Peel, remove stones and cut up the nectarines. In a blender or food processor, blend nectarines, stevia, and lemon juice until smooth. Divide berries among 4 sauce dishes. Pour on nectarine sauce, garnish, and serve.

Variations: Sprinkle on ground ginger or cinnamon.

Garlic and Yogurt Salad Dressing
Yields 1 cup dressing

Also perfect as a baked potato topper.

- 3/4 cup plain, low fat yogurt
- 1 small clove of garlic, minced, or garlic powder to taste
- 1/4 teaspoon crumbled dry basil
- 1/2 tablespoon seasoned rice vinegar
- 1/16 teaspoon Green Stevia Powder
- 1 teaspoon finely chopped fresh parsley
- 4 tablespoons sugarfree mayonnaise

Whisk together all ingredients. Pour into a small jar and cover. Chill overnight to blend flavors.

Basic Salad Dressing

Yields about 1 3/4 cups

A creamy, smooth sandwich spread or base for dressings.

- 2 tablespoons cornstarch OR arrowroot powder
- 1 1/4 cups water
- 1/4 teaspoons ground mustard
- 1/16 teaspoon garlic powder
- 1/4 teaspoon onion powder
- 1/4 to 1/2 teaspoon salt
- 1/16 teaspoon Stevia Extract Powder
- 2 tablespoons fresh lemon juice
- 1/2 teaspoon mashed, steamed carrot (for color)
- 1/4 cup vegetable oil

Stir together cornstarch and water in a medium saucepan. Cook over medium heat, stirring, until thickened. Set aside to cool to room temperature.

Spoon dressing into a blender bowl and add mustard, garlic powder, onion powder, salt, stevia, lemon juice, and carrot. Process until smooth. With blender operating at medium speed, gradually add oil. Spoon into a jar, cover and refrigerate. Dressing thickens as it chills.

Use within a week.

Orange Poppy Seed Dressing   Yields 1 1/4 cups

This orange-sparked dressing is impressive on fruit salads.

- 1 cup Basic Salad Dressing (see index)
- 1/4 teaspoon Stevia Extract Powder
- 1 teaspoon shredded orange peel
- 1/4 cup fresh orange juice
- 1/2 teaspoon poppy seeds

Whisk to combine all ingredients in a bowl. Store in a covered jar. Refrigerate and use within a week.

Creamy French Dressing   Yields about 1 cup

Complete your salad with this coloful, spicy dressing.

- 3 tablespoons fresh lemon juice
- 1/8 teaspoon Stevia Extract Powder
- 1/4 teaspoon paprika
- 1/4 teaspoon salt, optional
- 1/4 teaspoon ground mustard
- 1/8 teaspoon garlic powder
- 1/2 cup vegetable oil
- 1/4 cup Basic Salad Dressing (see index)
- 1 1/2 tablespoons Tomato Ketchup (see index)

Place all ingredients in a small, deep bowl and whisk together. Store in a covered jar and refrigerate.

Use within one week.

Ranch Dill Dressing

A flavor treat over steamed cauliflower or vegetable salads.

- 1/2 cup buttermilk
- 1/4 cup soft tofu
- 3 tablespoons Basic Salad Dressing (see index)
- 1/4 teaspoon Green Stevia Powder
- 1/2 to 1 teaspoon dry dill weed
- 3/4 teaspoon nutritional yeast flakes
- 1/2 teaspoon onion powder
- 1/4 teaspoon salt, optional
- 1/4 teaspoon crushed dry basil leaves

Whisk together all ingredients. Refrigerate in a covered jar. Use within a week.

Old Fashioned Cooked Salad Dressing
Yields 1 cup dressing

Use this tangy, sweet dressing for potato salad also.

- 1/2 tablespoon arrowroot powder or cornstarch
- 1/4 teaspoon Stevia Extract Powder
- 1/4 teaspoon salt (optional)
- 1/3 teaspoon dry mustard
- 3 tablespoons soy beverage powder or nonfat dry milk
- 3/4 cup water
- 2 egg yolks
- 1 tablespoon cider vinegar
- 3 tablespoons water

In a double boiler pan stir together arrowroot powder, stevia, salt, mustard, and soy powder. Drop egg yolks into water and beat briefly with a fork. Stir yolk mixture into the dry ingredients.

Place stirred mixture over simmering water and cook to thicken. Turn off heat and cook, stirring an additional minute. Remove from heat.

Stir together vinegar and the remaining 3 tablespoons water. Mix into the cooked dressing. Cool. Pour into jar, cover, and refrigerate.

Variation: For more "tang", use 2 tablespoons vinegar and reduce water to 2 tablespoons.

Tip: Use within 1 or 2 days.

Fresh Citrus Dressing

Yields 1 cup dressing

Grapefruit flavor gives zing to leafy greens or fruit salad.

- 1 pink grapefruit
- 1/16 teaspoon Stevia Extract Powder
- 1/2 teaspoon dry chopped or minced onion, optional

Squeeze the grapefruit. Pick out seeds and discard. Add pulp back to the juice making about 1 cup. Place in a small glass jar and stir in stevia and onion. Cover and refrigerate 1/2 hour before serving.

Chapter 7

Savory Sauces

Simmer some Spicy Applesauce on a chilly morning and enjoy the fragrance throughout the house. This tangy-sweet dessert is the perfect finish for a winter lunch. Some of the sauces are meant to be poured over desserts. Others can fill crepes, cream puffs, or cake rolls. Try pineapple sauce on Apple Pie, Cherry Sauce in Crepes or Cream Puffs. The Very Orange Sauce has an intense, sweet flavor.

The rich, red, tomato-based sauces are frequently used in recipes and at the table. Pesto Sauce gives marvelous herbal flavor to salads, pastas, breads, and more. Use the well-seasoned marinade for vegetables, chicken or pork—either to roast in the oven or for outdoor cookery.

Tomato Ketchup

Yields 1 pint ketchup

Thick and lightly spiced, with a rich tomato flavor.

- 2 3/4 cups home canned tomato puree or 2 cans (10 3/4 ounce) plain tomato puree
- 1/8 teaspoon allspice
- 1/4 teaspoon cinnamon
- 1/2 teaspoon dry mustard
- 1/8 to 1/4 teaspoon Stevia Extract Powder
- 1/2 teaspoon salt
- 1/4 teaspoon onion powder
- 1/8 teaspoon garlic powder
- 2 tablespoons cider vinegar

Homemade tomato puree needs to be as thick as store-bought applesauce. If yours is too thin, simmer over low heat to reduce before measuring. Mix all ingredients in a medium saucepan. Stir over moderate heat a few minutes until mixture bubbles up. Reduce heat to low and cover with a lid in a tilted position, allowing steam to escape.

Continue to cook and stir occasionally for 30 to 45 minutes or to thicken as desired.

Pour into a pint jar and cool to room temperature. Cover and refrigerate. Use within 2 weeks. Ketchup may also be frozen.

Tomato Style Barbecue Sauce
Yields 1/2 cup sauce

A robust sauce for the kitchen or outdoor barbecuing.

- 1/2 cup Tomato Ketchup (see index)
- 2 teaspoons prepared mustard or mustard blend
- 2 teaspoons fresh lemon juice
- 1/16 teaspoon Green Stevia Powder or a pinch of Stevia Extract Powder
- 1/2 teaspoon onion powder

Whisk all ingredients together. Refrigerate in a covered jar until ready to use.

Tips:
- On the outdoor grill, this sauce is great for barbecued chicken, pork chops, steak, or turkey loin chops
- In the kitchen use with meat loaf, sandwiches, meat balls, and more.

Pesto Sauce

Yields 1 cup sauce

This unique herbal sauce freezes well for later use.

- 1/2 cup parsley leaves, stems removed
- 3/4 cup chopped fresh basil leaves
- 1 clove garlic, peeled and chopped
- 1/4 cup vegetable oil (olive oil if you prefer)
- 1/16 teaspoon salt
- 1/8 teaspoon Green Stevia Powder
- 1/4 cup chopped walnuts
- 3 1/2 tablespoons Parmesan cheese or Parmesan style soy cheese

Process in a blender the parsley, garlic, oil, salt, and stevia. Push down the sauce with a rubber spatula as needed. ALWAYS SWITCH OFF APPLIANCE BEFORE INSERTING A UTENSIL. Add remaining ingredients and blend. The sauce need not be entirely smooth. Refrigerate in a covered jar.

Tip: Pesto Sauce adds quite a pleasing flavor to pasta, salads, breads, or main dishes. Use it with Whole Wheat Egg Noodles.

Barbecue Marinade

Yields marinade for 6 barbecue servings

Seasoned just right for barbecuing meats or vegetables.

- ½ cup safflower, canola, or olive oil
- 2 1/2 tablespoons fresh lemon juice
- 2 tablespoons lite soy sauce
- 1/2 teaspoon Green Stevia Powder
- 1 teaspoon sesame oil (from toasted sesame seeds)
- 1/4 teaspoon dry rosemary
- 2 teaspoons Garden Blend Seasoning (see index)
- 1 teaspoon dry basil leaves, crushed
- 1/2 teaspoon ready-to-use garlic (optional)

Mix all ingredients together in a deep bowl large enough to hold all the vegetables or meat to be barbecued. Cover with plastic wrap and refrigerate until needed.

Tips:
- For using fresh basil or rosemary, chop the leaves and use 3 times as much of the fresh herbs.
- Tofu can also marinate in this sauce before going into a stir-fry.

Pineapple Sauce

Yields 2 1/2 cups

This sauce is tasty over cakes and cobblers.

- 1 1/2 cups sugarfree pineapple juice
- 1 cup natural apple juice
- 2 tablespoons cornstarch or arrowroot powder
- 1/4 teaspoon Stevia Extract Powder

Place all ingredients in a medium saucepan. Cook and stir over medium heat until sauce thickens.

Good warm or chilled. For a thicker sauce increase the cornstarch to 2 1/2 tablespoons.

Variation: Stir a dash of cinnamon into the warm sauce for a different flavor.

Very Orange Sauce

Yields 1 cup

This colorful sauce is sweet and tangy.

- 1/8 teaspoon Stevia Extract Powder
- 1 tablespoon cornstarch or arrowroot powder
- 1 tablespoon fresh lemon juice
- 1/4 teaspoon dry lemon peel
- 1 cup unsweetened orange juice

Stir together cornstarch and stevia in a small saucepan. Add lemon juice, lemon peel, and orange juice. Bring to a boil over medium heat, stirring constantly. Cook until thickened. Remove from heat. Serve warm or pour into a jar, cover and refrigerate.

Variation: For a more intense orange flavor, add a couple drops of orange extract and omit the lemon peel.

Cherry Sauce

Yields about 2 1/2 cups

Use to fill cream puffs or make an ice cream sundae.

- 1 can (16 ounce) pitted red tart pie cherries, water pack OR 2 cups fresh cherries plus 1/2 cup water.
- 1 teaspoon Stevia Extract Powder
- 3/4 cup natural apple juice
- 3 tablespoons cornstarch or arrowroot powder
- 1/4 teaspoon almond extract

Drain cherry juice into a medium saucepan. Dissolve stevia in this juice. Add cherries and set aside 30 minutes to absorb sweetness.

Dissolve cornstarch in the apple juice. Bring cherries to a boil and stir in the cornstarch mixture. Reduce heat and simmer while the sauce thickens, stirring gently. Remove from heat and mix in the almond extract.

Serve at room temperature. Refrigerate leftovers.

Cranberry Applesauce

Yields 1-1/2 quarts

Tangy flavor and a rich red color.

- 3 cups cranberries (12 ounce), fresh or frozen
- 6 cups quartered, peeled apples (8 or 9 apples)
- 1 3/4 cups water
- 2 teaspoons Stevia Extract Powder

Place all ingredients into a large saucepan. Bring to a boil and then cook over low heat, stirring occasionally. When fruit is tender, cool to room temperature.

Refrigerate in a covered jar. For a smooth sauce, process in batches in a blender until smooth. Refrigerate.

Variation: For a spicy sauce, stir in 1/4 teaspoon cinnamon and dashes of nutmeg and allspice.

Spicy Applesauce

Yields 1 1/2 to 2 pints

This one is a tasty dish for breakfast, lunch, or dinner.

- 3 pounds apples (choose tart apples such as Granny Smith)
- 7 tablespoons lemon juice
- 1/2 teaspoon cinnamon
- 1/2 teaspoon nutmeg
- Dash of allspice
- 1 1/4 teaspoons Stevia Extract Powder
- 1 cup water, plus more as needed

Peel, core, and chop the apples. There should be 6 cups. Place in a large saucepan. Add lemon juice, spices, and stevia. Add just enough water to keep them from burning.

Cover and cook very slowly for 4 hours with the heat turned on low. Add water as necessary and stir occasionally, about every 20 minutes. Do not let the applesauce scorch!

Serve warm or chilled. Store leftovers in a covered jar and refrigerate.

Variation: Add 1/8 teaspoon molasses with spices if desired.

Fresh Applesauce

Use your favorite variety for this simple treat.

- 3 chilled apples, scrubbed
- 1/8 teaspoon Stevia Extract Powder
- 1/2 cup fruit juice such as orange or pineapple
- juice of 1/2 lemon or lime, optional.

Rinse, cut, and core apples. Place in the blender bowl together with stevia and fruit juice. Blend until smooth. Serve. Shake on some spices if you like.

Tip: Change the consistency by varying the amount of fruit juice.

Sweet Rhubarb Sauce

Yields 1 pint

This tangy sauce may be eaten plain or used in dessert recipes.

- 1 pound rhubarb, cut in 1 inch pieces
- 1/4 cup water
- 1 teaspoon Stevia Extract Powder

Place rhubarb, water, and stevia in a medium saucepan. Bring to a boil. Reduce heat and simmer 5 to 10 minutes or until rhubarb softens, stirring as needed.

Cool and refrigerate in a covered jar.

Fresh Strawberry Sauce

Yields 2 3/4 cups

Use this same recipe to make blueberry sauce!

- 3 1/2 cups sliced strawberries
- 1/2 teaspoon Stevia Extract Powder
- 1 teaspoon fresh lemon juice, optional

Place all ingredients in a food processor bowl or blender bowl. Process a few seconds or until smooth. Serve immediately.

If some sauce is left over, simmer over low heat about 5 minutes. Cool and refrigerate.

Tip: This bright red fruit sauce tastes delicious over pancakes or cheesecake.

Blackberry Sauce

Yields 1 pint

Add some berry pizazz to breakfast, lunch or dinner.

- 4 cups (16 ounces) fresh or frozen blackberries
- 1/3 cup water
- 1/3 teaspoon Stevia Extract Powder
- 4 teaspoons cornstarch OR arrowroot powder
- 1/3 cup water

Measure blackberries, water, and stevia into a medium saucepan. Bring to a boil, reduce heat and simmer 3 minutes.

Dissolve cornstarch in the remaining 1/3 cup water and stir into the cooking sauce. Continue to simmer another 2 minutes, stirring as needed. Serve warm or chilled. Refrigerate leftovers.

Variation: Stir in 1/16 teaspoon coriander or cinnamon.

Chapter 8

Sweet Toppings and Spreads

Strawberry Spread spooned over ice cream makes a luscious sundae. Bake a Jelly Roll and fill with Blueberry Jam. Surround with Whipped Cream rosettes. Decorate the top with Powdered Stevia Garnish sprinkled through a doily.

Whipped Cream is easy to prepare and a perfect touch for many desserts. Keep in mind that cream is high in fat.

Oat Cinnamon Crunch has proven to be a delicious convenience and was used liberally in the preparation of this book. It provides a nutty flavor and crunchy texture to a wide variety of desserts. Stored in a covered jar, this Crunch keeps for several weeks in a refrigerator.

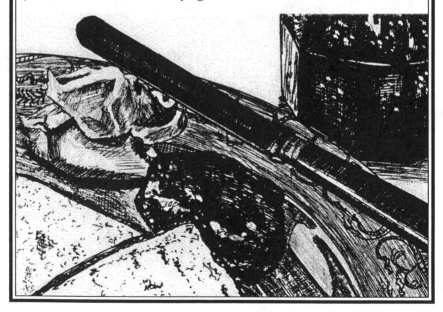

Strawberry Mango Jam

Yields about 1 pint

Spread your hot muffin or toast with this delightful, sweet jam.

- 3 cups sliced strawberries
- ¾ cup chopped mango
- 1 tablespoon fresh lemon juice
- ¾ to 1 teaspoon Stevia Extract Powder
- ¼ cup water

Place all ingredients in a saucepan over medium heat and bring to a boil. Reduce heat and simmer about 20 minutes, stirring as needed. If jam is too lumpy at this point, mash with a potato masher.

Continue to simmer another 30 minutes or until jam reaches the desired consistency. Pour into jar, cover, and refrigerate. Use within a week.

Apple Grape Jam

Use either gelatin or agar agar. Nicely spreadable.

- 2 cups natural grape juice (or 6 ounces frozen, unsweetened grape juice concentrate plus ¾ cup water)
- 1 teaspoon Stevia Extract Powder
- 1 envelope unflavored gelatin OR 2 tablespoons agar agar
- 1 cup unsweetened applesauce

In a medium saucepan, simmer natural grape juice until it is reduced to 1½ cups (or place frozen juice concentrate and water in pan). Stir in stevia. Sprinkle gelatin (or agar agar) over juice and allow to soften 5 minutes. Dissolve gelatin over low heat. If using agar agar, bring to a boil, then simmer 5 minutes, stirring as needed. Remove from heat and add the applesauce. Pour into jars. When partially gelled, stir once more, cover, and refrigerate.

Strawberry Spread

- 4 cups hulled and chopped strawberries
- 2 teaspoons fresh lemon juice
- 1½ teaspoons Stevia Extract Powder
- ¾ cup cold water
- 1 envelope unflavored gelatin OR 1½ tablespoons agar agar)

In a medium saucepan mash strawberries. Remove 1½ cups of the mashed berries and reserve. To the saucepan add lemon juice, stevia, water, and gelatin (or agar agar). Set aside for 5 minutes. Dissolve gelatin over low heat. If using agar agar, bring to a boil, then simmer 5 minutes, stirring as needed. Remove from heat and mix in remaining 1½ cups mashed berries. Pour into jars and cool to room temperature. Cover and refrigerate.

Peach Jam

Yields about 3 1/4 cups

This golden fruit spread is delicious on toast.

- 4 1/2 cups chopped peaches (about 8)
- 1/4 cup water
- 2 tablespoons agar agar OR 1 envelope unflavored gelatin
- 1 teaspoon Stevia Extract Powder
- 1 teaspoon fresh lemon juice
- 1/2 cup water
- few drops almond extract

Place peaches and 1/4 cup water in a medium saucepan. Simmer for 5 minutes.

Add agar agar (or gelatin), stevia, and lemon juice to the remaining 1/2 cup water. Set aside to soften for 5 minutes. Stir into peaches and bring to a boil. Reduce heat and simmer 5 minutes. Mash the peach mixture with a potato masher and stir in almond flavoring, if used. Cool to room temperature. Pour into jars, cover, and refrigerate.

Variation: Increase lemon juice to 1 tablespoon for more "Tang."

Blueberry Jam

Yields 1 1/2 to 2 cups

Taste the wonderful all-fruit flavor

- 1 pound fresh blueberries or sugarfree frozen blueberries, thawed
- 1 1/2 to 2 teaspoons Stevia Extract Powder
- 7 teaspoons fresh lemon juice

Place blueberries in a saucepan, mashing slightly with a potato masher. Simmer until soft, stirring occasionally. Dissolve stevia in lemon juice and stir into blueberries. Simmer until jam is thickened, about 30 to 40 minutes. Cool and refrigerate in a covered jar or store in a freezer.

Applebutter Now

Quick, easy, and delicious. Enjoy!

- 3 cups thick, unsweetened applesauce
- 1/16 teaspoon ground ginger
- 1 1/2 teaspoons cinnamon
- dash of cloves
- 1 or 2 teaspoons cider vinegar
- 1 teaspoon Stevia Extract Powder

If homemade applesauce is used it may need to be thicker. Simmer, uncovered, over low heat to the desired consistency. Stir spices, vinegar, and stevia into applesauce. Set aside 15 minutes. Whisk briefly to make sure it is well mixed. Pour into a quart jar, cover, and refrigerate. Allow flavors to mingle for one day. Use within a week or freeze for later use.

For already thick applesauce, no heating is necessary. The amounts of stevia, vinegar, and spices may be varied according to taste.

Whipped Cream

Yields 2 cups

The real thing. Great taste, but it does have real calories!

- 1 cup liquid whipping cream
- 1/4 teaspoon Stevia Extract Powder
- 1 teaspoon vanilla extract

Whip together all the ingredients in a small, deep mixing bowl until soft peaks form. Do not over-beat or it will become a bowl of lumps (sweet butter, actually).

Serve immediately or refrigerate.

Variation: Many spices and flavorings can be used. For example, try a dash of cinnamon with pumpkin pie or a few drops of almond flavoring to serve over peach cobbler.

Fluffy Vanilla Whip
Yields 2 1/2 cups (or 1 1/4 cups in agar agar version)

This low fat, versatile topping is rich in flavor and holds up well in the refrigerator.

- 2/3 cup water (or 3/4 cup water for agar agar version)
- 1 teaspoon unflavored gelatin (or 2 teaspoons agar agar)
- 1/2 cup nonfat dry milk
- 1 1/2 teaspoons vanilla extract
- dash of salt, optional
- 1/2 teaspoon Stevia Extract Powder
- 3 tablespoons vegetable oil

Measure water into a small, deep stainless steel mixing bowl. Sprinkle in gelatin and allow to soften 5 minutes. Place bowl over low heat and stir to dissolve gelatin. (For agar agar, soften in water using a small saucepan. Bring to a boil, reduce to simmer and cook 5 minutes.)

Stir in dry milk, vanilla extract, salt, and stevia. Chill to unbeaten eggwhite consistency (or firmer for agar agar), then beat 4 minutes. Gradually add oil while beating an additional minute. Mixture will be light and fluffy. Refrigerate. Stir briefly before serving.

Tips:
- For a meringue-like pie topping, spread freshly whipped topping over chilled pie and sprinkle with toasted, unsulphured coconut. Refrigerate.
- Use a pastry bag with a decorative tip to pipe topping on pies or cakes. Refrigerate
- Vary flavor by adding spices.

Oat Cinnamon Crunch Yields 2 3/4 cups

An easy way to add a delicious crunch to desserts.

- 1 cup whole wheat pastry flour
- 1/2 teaspoon Stevia Extract Powder OR 1 1/2 teaspoons Green Stevia Powder
- 1/2 teaspoon cinnamon
- dash of cloves (optional)
- 2/3 cup rolled oats
- 1/2 cup chopped walnuts
- 1/2 cup non-hydrogenated margarine

Lightly oil a 9 x 13 inch baking pan. Stir together flour, stevia, and spices. Add oats and walntus, then mix. Stir in margarine and press into the oiled pan. Bake in a preheated 350 degree oven for 10 to 15 minutes or until lightly browned.

Cool the pan on a wire rack. Using a wide spatula, transfer the topping into a jar. Cover. Use within a few days or refrigerator.

Powdered Stevia Garnish Yield: Garnishes 12 desserts

An easy decoration for desserts.

- 2 tablespoons cornstarch or arrowroot powder
- 1/8 teaspoon Stevia Extract Powder

Thoroughly mix together the 2 ingredients. Spoon into a small jar, cover, and store on a cabinet shelf.

To use, spoon 1/2 **teaspoon garnish** into a mesh tea strainer and gently shake over the surface of the dessert. For a decorative touch, place a paper or plastic doily atop the dessert and sift on the Stevia Garnish. Lift the doily to reveal a lovely pattern.

Chapter 9

Tempting Main Dishes

In main dishes, Green Stevia Powder really shines as a flavor enhancer. Anywhere from a pinch to 1/4 teaspoon of the sweet green powder will bring out other flavors in a subtle way. Sometimes you'll need to use less of the other seasonings in your own standby recipes.

A set of measuring spoons including a 1/8 teaspoon is convenient. It's easy to measure 1/16 teaspoon by using half of the 1/8 amount.

Seasonings in these dishes, though diverse, are the ones relished by our tasting panel. You are the expert on seasonings your family enjoys, so do adjust to include family favorites. A good procedure is to first prepare the recipe as written, then experiment and make changes.

Sweet Potato Casserole

Golden sweet potatoes, tart apples, and herbs combine for a savory main dish.

- 4 cups sweet potatoes, about 2 medium potatoes, in 3/4 inch cubes
- 2/3 cup onion cubes
- 3 tablespoons tangerine or orange juice
- 1/4 teaspoon Stevia Extract Powder
- 1/4 teaspoon salt
- 1 tablespoon fresh lime or lemon Juice
- 1 1/2 tablespoons vegetable oil
- 2 1/2 cups tart apples, such as Winesap, cubed
- 1 teaspoon Garden Blend Seasoning (see index)

Lightly oil a large casserole or 9 x 13 inch baking pan. Pile sweet potatoes and onions in the casserole.

Stir together the tangerine juice, stevia, salt, lime juice, and oil. Pour this mixture over the sweet potatoes and onions. Stir to combine. Cover casserole and bake in a preheated 350 degree oven for 25 minutes.

Remove casserole from oven, stir in apples and sprinkle with seasoning. Cook, uncovered, another 20 minutes. Serve hot.

Maple Glazed Loin Chops

Juicy apples and pears team with tender chops.

- 4 small pork loin chops (about 16 to 18 ounces total)
- 1/3 cup Maple Apple Syrup (see index)
- 1 1/2 tablespoons prepared mustard or mustard blend
- 1/2 teaspoon dry rosemary
- 1/4 teaspoon Green Stevia Powder
- 1/4 teaspoon ready-to-use chopped garlic
- 2 ripe yellow pears
- 2 tart apples
- 5 tablespoons Maple Apple Syrup
- parsley sprigs for garnish (optional)

Lightly oil a 9 inch square baking dish. Trim obvious fat from the chops. Combine the 1/3 cup of Maple Apple Syrup, mustard, rosemary, stevia, and garlic in a small bowl. Spoon over the chops in the baking dish and bake in a preheated oven set at 400 degrees for 30 minutes. Chops should be tender and no longer pink.

Peel, core, and thickly slice apples and pears. Using 1 tablespoon oil in a large skillet, saute fruit about 5 minutes. Add the 5 tablespoons syrup and simmer, stirring as needed for about 8 minutes.

Serve with garnish as desired.

Herbed Fillet of Pollock

Topped with a basil onion sauce and crisp rye croutons.

- 1/2 pound pollock fillets
- 2 tablespoons butter
- 3 tablespoons sweet red pepper, chopped
- 1/2 onion, chopped
- 1 1/2 tablespoons chopped fresh basil leaves
- 1/4 cup low fat yogurt
- 1/16 teaspoon Green Stevia Powder
- 1 1/2 tablespoons seasoned rice vinegar
- 1 tablespoon vegetable oil
- 1 clove garlic, peeled and thinly sliced
- 1/4 cup rye bread cubes

Butter a deep pie dish and place the pollock fillets in it in a single layer.

Melt the 2 tablespoons butter in a skillet over medium heat and saute pepper and onion for 5 minutes. Stir in basil and spoon mixture over the fish.

Combine yogurt, stevia, and vinegar, then pour this mixture over the fillets and herbs.

Place the oil in the skillet and briefly cook garlic to soften. Add the bread cubes to the pan, stirring to toast. Spoon atop the fish and bake in a 350 degree preheated oven for 35 minutes.

Variation: This recipe can be used for other kinds of filleted fish as well.

Sweet 'N Sour Vegetable Pork Stir Fry
Yields 5 servings

Browned meat compliments the sweet-sour vegetable blend.

- 1/4 cup orange juice
- 1/4 cup water
- 1/4 teaspoon Stevia Extract Powder
- 1 tablespoon seasoned rice vinegar
- 1 tablespoon cider vinegar
- 1/4 teaspoon garlic powder
- 1 tablespoon lite soy sauce
- 1 tablespoon arrowroot powder or cornstarch
- 8 ounces boneless pork loin cut in bite size pieces
- 2 tablespoons vegetable oil
- 1/2 cup chopped onion
- 2 cups sugar snap peas or snow peas (about 6 ounces)
- 1/2 cup red bell pepper cut in julienne pieces
- 2 cups chopped red or green cabbage
- 1 1/2 cups sliced button mushrooms (about 4 ounces)
- 3 cups cooked brown rice
- 1/2 teaspoon Garden Blend Herbal Seasoning, optional (see index)
- ground ginger

Combine the first 8 ingredients for sauce in a pint jar. Cover securely and shake to combine. Set aside.

Using a large skillet, brown the pork in oil. Add onion and stir, cooking, until meat is well browned and no longer pink. Stir in peas, peppers, and cabbage, then cook another 5 minutes. Add mushrooms and heat through. Pour sauce over the stir fry. Stir and cook briefly while cornstarch thickens.

Combine seasonings with rice. Serve stir fry over rice and season with ginger as desired.

Roasted Squash Onion Pie

Yields 6 servings

Crisp rice crust filled with savory herbed vegetables.

- 2 large egg whites, lightly beaten
- 2 cups cooked brown rice
- 3 tablespoons grated Parmesan cheese OR Parmesan style soy cheese.
- 4 cups sliced squash
- 1 1/2 cups thinly sliced onions
- 1/8 teaspoon salt (optional)
- 1 teaspoon chopped ready-to-use garlic
- 1 1/4 teaspoons crushed dry basil
- 1 teaspoon dry oregano
- 1 1/2 tablespoons vegetable oil
- 1/4 teaspoon Green Stevia Powder
- 4 Roma tomatoes, sliced
- 1/4 cup black olives, sliced (optional)
- 2/3 cup grated mozzarella cheese OR mozzarella style soy cheese.

Stir together egg whites, rice, and Parmesan cheese. Press into a 9 inch, oiled pie dish. Bake in a preheated 400 degree oven for 12 minutes.

On an oiled cookie sheet pile the squash, onion, salt, garlic, and spices. Dissolve stevia in oil. Stir into the vegetable mixture, spread on cookie sheet, and bake 10 minutes at 400 degrees. Stir vegetables and bake another 10 minutes. Add tomatoes and olives. Toss to mix.

Spread 1/3 cup of the mozzarella cheese on the crust. Top with vegetables and remaining 1/3 cup cheese. Bake at 375 degrees for 30 minutes. Serve hot.

Tip: Try tomato Ketchup (see index) on the pie.

Mom's Chicken Noodle Soup   Yields 5 servings

A hearty soup rich with herbs and chunks of chicken.

- 1 tablespoon butter
- 3/4 cup chopped summer squash
- 3/4 cup chopped carrots
- 1/4 cup chopped celery
- 1 tablespoon cornstarch
- 1/2 cup water
- 1/8 teaspoon Green Stevia Powder
- 2 cups chicken broth or Savory Vegetable Stock (see index)
- 1/2 to 1 teaspoon dry crushed basil
- 1 tablespoon dry onion flakes
- salt and pepper (optional)
- 1 1/2 cups Whole Wheat Egg Noodles (see index)
- 1/2 pound boned, skinned chicken breast (cut in ½ inch pieces)
- 2 tablespoons chopped parsley

Melt butter in a large saucepan over medium heat. Add squash, carrots, and celery, then saute for 5 minutes. Mix cornstarch, water, and stevia, then stir into the vegetables. Add broth, basil, onion, salt, and pepper, if used. Bring to a boil. Reduce heat to a simmer, cover, and cook 5 minutes.

Add noodles and chicken. Bring to a boil. Reduce heat, cover, and simmer 10 minutes. Stir in parsley. Serve.

Whole Wheat Egg Noodles

Yields 4 servings

This versatile pasta is delicious in soups or casseroles.

- 1 3/4 cups whole wheat pastry flour
- 1/16 teaspoon Green Stevia Powder
- 2 tablespoons arrowroot powder or cornstarch
- 1/2 teaspoon salt, optional
- 2 eggs
- 3 tablespoons cold water
- 2 tablespoons vegetable oil
- additional arrowroot powder or cornstarch

Using a medium bowl mix together the dry ingredients. In a separate bowl whisk the liquid ingredients. Combine the 2 mixtures. Stir to form a stiff dough and then knead for 5 minutes – this can be done directly in the bowl. Wrap dough in plastic wrap and set aside for 1 hour at room temperature.

Sprinkle arrowroot powder on a clean surface to roll out dough. Using 1/2 of the dough roll it to a 15 inch circle. Cut into 4 strips and then cut crosswise into 1/4 inch noodles. Repeat with remaining dough.

Spread noodles on clean towels to dry 1 hour or longer. Cook at this point or refrigerate in a covered container. They may also be frozen for later use.

To cook noodles simmer in seasoned broth or vegetable stock a few minutes as desired.

Barbecued Vegetables

Choose other vegetables if you wish.

- 1 recipe Barbecue Marinade (see index)
- 2 bell peppers, any color, quartered or cut smaller
- 4 small zucchini squash, cut in 1 inch sections
- 8 ounces mushrooms (cut in half if large)
- 4 carrots, cut in 1/2 inch sections

Toss vegetables in the marinade making sure they get well coated. Cover the bowl with plastic wrap and refrigerate for 3 to 6 hours. Stir once each hour.

For oven barbecuing, lift vegetables into a shallow baking dish. Bake in a preheated oven at 375 degrees for 30 to 45 minutes or until tender.

Follow manufacturer's directions when using a grill. For kabobs, thread marinated vegetables on skewers and heat, turning often, until tender. Remaining marinade can be used to dip or pour over vegetables in a serving dish.

Sunny Corn Casserole   Yields 5 Servings

Corn and savory vegetables baked in a custard base.

- 1 tablespoon butter or vegetable oil
- 1/4 cup chopped fresh mushrooms
- 2/3 cup chopped red bell peppers
- 2/3 cup chopped onions
- 1 tablespoon finely chopped fresh parsley
- 1/2 cup yogurt or 1/3 cup soymilk
- 2 tablespoons whole wheat flour or barley flour
- 2 eggs
- 1 can (15 ounce) whole kernel corn with liquid, or 2 cups fresh corn plus 1/2 cup water.
- 1/2 teaspoon dry basil leaves
- 1/8 teaspoon Green Stevia Powder
- 2 tablespoons toasted wheat germ or 1/2 cup whole wheat bread crumbs
- 1 1/2 to 2 tablespoons grated Parmesan cheese OR Parmesan style soy cheese.
- parsley and red pepper for garnish

Place butter in a small skillet. Lightly cook mushrooms, pepper, and onion about 7 minutes or until slightly softened, stirring as needed. Set aside.

Stir together parsley, yogurt, flour, eggs, corn, basil, and stevia. Add cooked vegetables and mix. Turn into an oiled 8 inch square baking dish. Sprinkle with wheat germ and cheese.

Bake in a 350 degree preheated oven for 35 to 40 minutes or until set. Garnish and serve.

Chapter 10
Old Fashioned Cookies

From crisp Maple Nut Cookies to moist Prune Nut Bars, Cookies are great as dessert fare or for handy snacking.

Be sure to refrigerate leftover moist cookies such as the Apple Bars. Store drier cookies in airtight containers at room temperature.

When a recipe calls for softened butter, remove it from the refrigerator one or two hours ahead of baking time.

Most high fat content cookies are baked on un-greased cookie sheets. Bar cookies require well-oiled pans for ease of removal.

Have some Stevia Sweet cookies and enjoy break time. When visiting friends, take along cookies in a decorated box to present to your hostess. Happy baking!

Spiced Holiday Cookies Yields 20 (2¾ inch) cookies

Cut these rolled cookies into holiday shapes and DECORATE!

- 1 cup whole wheat pastry flour
- ½ cup barley flour OR other whole grain flour
- 1½ teaspoons Stevia Extract Powder
- ½ teaspoon salt
- ¾ teaspoon ground ginger
- ¾ teaspoon cinnamon
- ⅛ teaspoon cloves
- 1 teaspoon baking powder
- ¼ cup butter, softened
- 3 tablespoons vegetable oil

Stir together the dry ingredients.

In a separate bowl beat remaining ingredients. Add the flour mixture and stir just to combine. Roll out dough to ⅛ inch thickness on a floured surface. Cut and place on lightly oiled baking sheets. Bake at 375 degrees from 7 to 10 minutes. Watch carefully. Cookies will be lightly browned on the bottom. Cool on racks.

Decorate as desired.

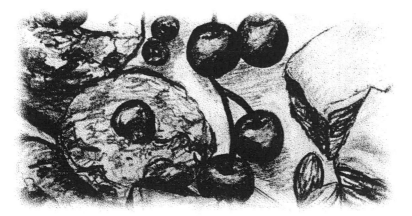

Peanut Butter Fruit Bars

Yields 36 cookies

A crunchy carob layer tops these oat and fruit cookie bars OR use other chips on top for a flavor twist.

- 1/4 cup natural applesauce
- 3/4 teaspoon Stevia Extract Powder
- 1 teaspoon vanilla extract
- 2/3 cup natural peanut butter
- 3/4 cup chopped dates
- 1/2 cup chopped pecans
- 1/4 cup nonfat dry milk, or more for firmer cookies
- 2 tablespoons softened butter
- 2/3 cup rolled oats
- 2 tablespoons butter
- 1 cup sugarfree carob chips

Measure applesauce, stevia, and vanilla extract into a medium bowl and stir with a wooden spoon. Add peanut butter, dates, pecans, dry milk, and 2 tablespoons butter. Mix well.

Toast rolled oats in a heavy skillet over medium heat about 6 minutes. Stir often. Oats will darken only slightly. Combine with applesauce mixture and press into an 8 inch square dish.

Use same skillet to melt 2 tablespoons butter over low heat. Evenly sprinkle in carob chips and allow to melt about half way. Do not stir. Slip the partially melted mass atop the cookie mixture and spread. Cool.

Variation: Simply sprinkle 1/2 cup carob chips over cookie bars without melting. Press in with a spatula. Cut and serve.

Fudgy Brownies

Yields 16 brownies

Fudge type moist carob cookie bars.

- 1 cup sugarfree carob chips
- 1/2 cup butter
- 1/2 cup plus 1 tablespoon whole wheat pastry flour
- 1 teaspoon Stevia Extract Powder OR 3 teaspoons Green Stevia Powder
- 1/4 teaspoon cinnamon
- shake each of nutmeg and allspice
- 1 teaspoon baking soda
- 2 eggs lightly beaten
- 2 teaspoons vanilla extract
- 1/2 teaspoon black walnut flavoring
- 4 tablespoons plain low fat yogurt OR 3 tablespoons soymilk
- 1/2 cup rolled oats, lightly chopped in a blender.
- 1/2 cup chopped walnuts

Oil a 9 inch square baking pan. Place chips and butter in a double boiler pan over boiling water. Turn heat to medium low. Stir occasionally and heat to melt most of the chips.

While chips are melting, mix flour, stevia, spices, and baking soda in a medium bowl. In a second bowl, combine eggs, extracts, and yogurt. Add chopped oats and set aside 15 minutes.

Remove carob mixture from heat. Quickly stir in dry ingredients and egg mixture. Turn into the prepared pan. Sprinkle walnuts over the surface and press in lightly with a spatula.

Bake in a 325 degree preheated oven for 16 to 19 minutes. Brownies should pull away from the sides of the pan. Do not overcook. Cool on a wire rack. Cut into squares.

Variation: For a drier bar, add an additional 2 tablespoons flour.

Prune Nut Bars

Yields 25 bars

These cookies require only 5 tablespoons of oil.

- 1/2 cup chopped dates
- 1 cup chopped, unsulphured prunes
- 3/4 cup water
- 1 teaspoon vanilla extract
- 1/2 teaspoon butterscotch flavoring
- 1 1/2 cups barley flour
- 1 teaspoon Stevia Extract Powder OR 3 teaspoons Green Stevia Powder
- 1/2 teaspoon salt
- 3/4 teaspoon baking soda
- 1/2 teaspoon cinnamon
- 1 1/2 cups rolled oats, lightly chopped in a blender
- 1/2 teaspoon butterscotch flavoring
- 1 teaspoon vanilla extract
- 1/2 cup plain low fat yogurt or 1/3 cup soymilk
- 5 tablespoons vegetable oil
- 1/2 cup finely chopped pecans

Combine dates, prunes, and water in small saucepan and bring to a boil. Reduce heat, stir as needed, and simmer to thicken a bit. Remove from heat and mash with a potato masher. Stir in 1 teaspoon vanilla extract and 1/2 teaspoon butterscotch flavoring.

Combine flour, stevia, salt, soda, and cinnamon. In separate bowl mix 1/2 teaspoon butterscotch flavoring and 1 teaspoon vanilla extract with yogurt, oil, and pecans. Add oats & set aside 15 minutes. With a fork, stir into dry ingredients. Mixture will be crumbly.

Lightly oil a 9 inch square baking dish. Firmly press half the cookie dough into the prepared pan. Spread with prune filling. Crumble remaining cookie dough over the filling. Bake in a preheated 350 degree oven for 22 to 25 minutes. Cookies will be lightly browned. Cool and cut into squares. Refrigerate leftovers or wrap individually in waxed paper and freeze.

Variations:
- Additional vanilla extract can replace butterscotch flavoring.
- Reduce salt to ¼ teaspoon or omit altogether.

Apple Bars

Very moist, chewy squares. Lightly spiced.

- 1/4 cup butter, softened
- 3 tablespoons vegetable oil.
- 3/4 teaspoon Stevia Extract Powder
- 1 teaspoon vanilla extract
- 2 eggs
- 1 cup plus 1 tablespoon whole wheat pastry flour
- 1/4 teaspoon salt
- 1 teaspoon cinnamon
- 1/8 teaspoon nutmeg
- 1 teaspoon baking powder
- 1 1/3 cups grated apples
- 1/3 cup chopped walnuts

In a medium bowl beat together butter, oil, stevia, vanilla extract, and eggs. Sift or stir together dry ingredients and stir into the butter mixture using a mixing spoon. Add apples and nuts and mix in. Batter will be stiff. Turn into oiled and floured 9 inch square baking dish. Cook at 350 degrees for 35 to 37 minutes in a preheated oven. Cool about 10 minutes and then cut into bars. Serve warm or cooled. Refrigerate leftovers.

Favorite Chip Cookies

Use the chips of your choice!

- 1 cup plus 2 tablespoons whole wheat pastry flour
- 1 1/2 teaspoons Stevia Extract Powder
- 1/4 teaspoon salt
- 2 cups rolled oats
- 1 teaspoon baking soda
- 1 cup hot water
- 1/2 cup vegetable oil.
- 1 teaspoon vanilla extract
- 1 teaspoon butterscotch flavoring
- 1 cup sugarfree carob chips
- 2 tablespoons sesame seeds OR 1/4 cup chopped walnuts

In a mixing bowl thoroughly combine flour, stevia, and salt. Set aside.

Chop oats in a blender until flakes are about half size. Pour hot water over baking soda and oats in a medium mixing bowl and beat to combine. Add oil, vanilla extract, and butterscotch flavoring. Add dry ingredients and stir well. Mix in carob chips and sesame seeds.

Using 2 teaspoons of dough per cookie, roll into balls and place on lightly oiled cookie sheets. Bake in a preheated oven at 325 degrees for 13 to 15 minutes. Cookies will be lightly browned on the bottom. Cool on racks and store in an airtight container.

Variation:
- Use chips of your choice in place of carob chips.

Maple Nut Cookies

Yields 30 to 35 cookies

Crisp, tasty, maple flavored nuggets.

- 3 tablespoons vegetable oil
- 1/4 cup butter
- 1 egg
- 1 teaspoon natural maple flavoring
- 2 tablespoons water
- 1 cup plus 1 tablespoon whole wheat flour
- 1 teaspoon Stevia extract Powder
- 1/4 teaspoon baking powder
- 1 cup unsulphured, flaked coconut
- 1 cup finely chopped walnuts

In a medium mixing bowl beat together oil, butter, egg, and flavoring until mixed. Stir in water.

Sift or stir together flour, stevia, and baking powder. With mixer beat half the dry ingredients into the butter mixture. Stir in remaining dry ingredients using a mixing spoon.

Chop coconut briefly in a blender or food processor. Add, together with nuts, to cookie dough and stir in. Mixture will be stiff. Drop by rounded teaspoonful onto greased cookie sheets and flatten a bit with fingers.

Bake in preheated 350 degree oven 10 minutes. Leave cookies on baking sheets 2 minutes. Remove to racks to finish cooling. Store in covered container.

Variations:
- 1 1/2 teaspoons vanilla extract can replace maple flavoring.
- Unsalted butter can be used.

Raisin Drop Cookies

Yields 55 Cookies

Make extras and freeze for snacking on later!

- 1 cup whole wheat pastry flour
- 1 teaspoon cinnamon
- 1/2 teaspoon nutmeg
- 1/4 teaspoon salt
- 1 1/4 to 1 1/2 teaspoons Stevia Extract Powder
- 1/4 cup finely chopped walnuts
- 3/4 cup raisins
- 3/4 cup water
- 1 teaspoon baking soda
- 4 or 5 tablespoons vegetable oil
- 1/4 cup sugarfree applesauce
- 2 teaspoons vanilla extract
- 1/4 cup milk, soymilk, or rice beverage.
- 2 cups rolled oats, coarsely chopped in a blender

In a medium mixing bowl thoroughly combine flour, spices, salt, and stevia. Stir in walnuts.

Place raisins and water in a small saucepan. Bring to a boil, turn off heat, and leave on the burner 10 minutes (or with a gas range, leave on very low heat). Drain raisins and add hot water, if necessary, to make ½ cup liquid. Place baking soda in a medium mixing bowl and stir in hot raisin liquid. Mix in vegetable oil, applesauce, vanilla extract, and milk. Stir in oats and set aside 15 minutes. Add raisins.

Drop by teaspoons on lightly oiled cookie sheets. Bake at 350 degrees in a preheated oven for 10 to 13 minutes or until lightly browned. Cool on racks and store in airtight containers.

Peanut Butter Cookies

Yields about 55 cookies

This cookie is perfect for freezing.

- 6 tablespoons vegetable oil
- 1/2 cup natural peanut butter at room temperature
- 2 eggs
- 1 1/2 teaspoon vanilla extract
- 2 teaspoons butterscotch flavoring
- 1/2 cup water
- 2 cups plus 2 tablespoons whole wheat flour
- 2 teaspoons Stevia Extract Powder
- 1/2 teaspoon baking powder
- 1 3/4 cups unsulphured, flaked coconut

In a medium mixing bowl beat together oil, peanut butter, eggs, vanilla extract, and butterscotch flavoring until mixed. Stir in water.

Sift or stir together flour, stevia, and baking powder. Beat half of the dry ingredients into the peanut butter mixture. Stir in the remaining dry ingredients using a mixing spoon.

Briefly chop coconut in a blender or food processor. Stir into the cookie dough; mixture will be stiff. Drop by the rounded teaspoons onto un-greased cookie sheets. Flatten with a fork.

Bake in a preheated oven at 350 degrees for 9 or 10 minutes. Leave cookies on baking sheet 2 minutes to cool. Remove to racks to finish cooling. Store in an airtight container.

Cashew Cookies

Yields 24 cookies

This chilled cookie features a nutty blend of flavors.

- 1/4 cup unsweetened coconut meal
- 1/2 cup unsweetened cashew butter
- 1/2 teaspoon butterscotch flavor
- 1/2 teaspoon vanilla extract
- 1/4 teaspoon Stevia Extract Powder OR ¾ teaspoon Green Stevia Powder
- 1/2 cup well chopped raw unsalted sunflower seeds
- 2 tablespoons soy beverage powder
- 1 tablespoon carob powder

Place coconut meal in a shallow bowl. Stir remaining ingredients together in mixing bowl in the order given. Chill briefly if mixture is too soft to form balls.

For each small cookie use 2 level teaspoons of cookie mixture. Roll in balls and coat with coconut meal. Flatten to a 1 1/2 inch disk. Place in a flat storage container and chill.

Variations:
- Omit butterscotch flavoring and increase vanilla extract to 1 teaspoon.
- Add 2 tablespoons sesame seeds.

Chapter 11

Irresistible Cakes

Cakes baked with stevia are sweet and special. These tips will help you along the way.

- *Pan size matters. To use a different size, adjust the time baked and perhaps the temperature.*
- *There is no need to sift flour before measuring.*
- *Prepare cake pans as specified in the recipes. Usually this is by oiling and dusting with flour.*
- *Only ground spices are used.*
- *Start preheating the oven 7 to 10 minutes before baking.*
- *Cakes "test done" when:*
  - *a. A wooden toothpick or knife inserted near the center comes out clean or*
  - *b. The cake springs back when lightly touched or*
  - *c. The cake slightly pulls away from the pan.*
- *Some Stevia Sweet cakes improve in flavor after standing overnight.*

Chocolate Date Cake
Yields 2 (8 inch) layers or a 9 x 13 inch loaf

Rich, dark cake with a moist and fluffy texture.

- 1 1/4 cups water
- 8 ounces dry, pitted dates
- 1 1/4 cups whole wheat pastry flour
- 1 1/4 cups unbleached white flour
- 1/2 cup cocoa powder
- 1/4 cup buttermilk powder
- 2 teaspoons baking powder
- 1 1/2 teaspoon baking soda
- 1 1/2 teaspoon Stevia Extract Powder
- 1/2 cup butter, softened
- 2/3 cup natural applesauce
- 1 teaspoon vanilla extract
- 3 large eggs
- 1/2 cup chopped pecans, optional

In a saucepan bring water to a boil. Remove from heat, add dates and cover. Cool. Puree dates and water. Set aside.

Stir together flours, cocoa, buttermilk powder, baking powder, baking soda, and stevia in a bowl. Set aside. Preheat oven to 350 degrees.

In a large bowl beat butter, applesauce, and vanilla extract until fluffy. Beat in eggs until thoroughly mixed Add the date puree and half the dry ingredients. Beat just until combined. By hand, stir in remaining dry ingredients and nuts.

Spread batter in oiled and floured pans. Bake 30 to 35 minutes or until cake tests done with a toothpick. Cool 5 minutes in layer pans and then turn out on racks or leave cake in the 9 x 13 inch pan. Frost as desired.

Date Spice Cake

Top this fruit filled cake with cinnamon frosting or whipped cream (see index).

- 2 7/8 cups whole wheat pastry flour
- 1 1/4 teaspoons Stevia Extract Powder
- 2 teaspoons baking powder
- 1 teaspoon baking soda
- 1 teaspoon cinnamon
- 1/4 teaspoon nutmeg
- 1/8 teaspoon cloves
- 3/4 cup mashed banana
- 1/2 cup well butter, well softened
- 1 teaspoon vanilla extract
- 3 large eggs
- 1 1/4 cups water
- 1 1/2 cups chopped, unsulphured dates
- 1/2 cup chopped, unsulphured prunes
- 1/2 cup chopped pecans

Stir together the dry ingredients.

In a medium mixing bowl beat together bananas, butter, and vanilla extract. Mix in eggs, half the dry ingredients, and half the water. By hand, stir in the remaining dry ingredients, water, chopped fruit, and nuts.

Pour into an oiled and floured 9 x 13 inch baking pan. Bake at 350 degrees in a preheated oven for 28 to 30 minutes or until cake tests done. Cool on a rack. This cake is delicious warm or cold and keeps well 2 or 3 days.

Banana Cake

Stays moist and flavorful.

- 3 cups whole wheat pastry flour
- 1/4 teaspoon salt
- 1 1/2 teaspoons Stevia Extract Powder
- 4 1/4 teaspoons baking powder
- 3 eggs, separated, at room temperature
- 1 cup soymilk or dairy milk
- 6 tablespoons vegetable oil
- 2 1/2 teaspoons vanilla extract
- 1 cup mashed ripe banana (about 2 bananas)
- frosting as desired (see index)
- 1/2 cup chopped walnuts

In a bowl sift or stir together the dry ingredients

Beat egg whites until stiff. Set aside.

Stir together egg yolks, soymilk, vegetable oil, vanilla extract, and banana. Add the dry ingredients and beat to combine. Fold in beaten egg whites.

Turn into 2 (8 inch diameter) oiled and floured cake pans. Bake in a preheated 350 degree oven 25 to 30 minutes or until cake tests done. Cool cake 10 minutes in pans. Turn out to finish cooling on racks.

Frost, then press nuts into the frosting.

Variations: Salt may be omitted.

Carob Prune Cake

Yields a 9 inch cake

A dark, rich cake. No need to frost.

- 1 cup water
- 1 cup pitted, chopped, unsulphured prunes
- 1/2 cup butter, softened
- 1 teaspoon Stevia Extract Powder
- 1 egg
- 1 cup whole wheat pastry flour
- 1/3 cup oat flour
- 1/3 cup carob powder
- 1 1/4 teaspoons baking soda
- 1/2 teaspoon cinnamon
- 1/4 teaspoon salt
- 1/4 cup soymilk or rice beverage

In a medium saucepan bring water and prunes to a boil. Simmer to soften prunes, about 5 minutes, stirring as needed. Mash briefly with a potato masher.

Beat butter and stevia in a medium bowl. Add eggs and prunes.

Combine dry ingredients and beat into prune mixture together with the soymilk. Batter will be thick.

Turn into an oiled and floured 9 inch square cake pan, spreading batter to the edges. Bake at 350 degrees in a preheated oven 23 to 25 minutes. Cool in pan 10 minutes and finish cooling on a rack.

Variations:

- 1 or 2 tablespoons of the carob powder may be replaced with whole wheat pastry flour.
- Chopped nuts (1/2 cup) can be stirred into the batter.

Strawberry Shortcake

Coconut adds a nice flavor to this popular dessert.

- 2 pints fresh strawberries, hulled and sliced
- 1/2 teaspoon Stevia Extract Powder
- 1 tablespoon water
- 1 teaspoon lemon juice
- 2 cups whole wheat pastry flour
- 1/8 teaspoon salt
- 4 teaspoons baking powder
- dash cinnamon or nutmeg
- 1/4 teaspoon Stevia Extract Powder
- 1/2 cup butter
- 2 large eggs, separated
- 1/2 cup milk
- 1/4 cup coconut meal
- 1 recipe Whipped Cream (see index)

Dissolve 1/2 teaspoon stevia in water and lemon juice; stir in strawberries and refrigerate.

Combine flour, salt, baking powder, spice, and the remaining 1/4 teaspoon stevia in a medium mixing bowl. Cut in butter. With a fork mix egg yolks and milk briefly; stir into flour mixture just to combine. Make 2 balls and press onto lightly oiled 8 inch layer pans. Beat egg whites as for meringue; spread half over each layer. Sprinkle with coconut meal. Bake in preheated 300 degree oven 25 minutes. Cool 15 minutes in pans; finish cooling on racks.

On serving plate spread one layer with Whipped Cream. Top with 1/2 of the berries. Place the other layer on top and finish with Whipped Cream and berries. Serve. Refrigerate leftovers.

Variations:
- Unsalted butter can be used.
- Banana cake (see index) can also be used with strawberries for a similar dessert that would yield 10 servings.

110

Jelly Roll Yields 10 servings

Choose your favorite filling for this elegant cake.

- 5 eggs, separated
- 1/4 cup water
- 1 teaspoon vanilla
- 1 teaspoon baking powder
- 3/4 cup unbleached white flour
- 1 1/4 teaspoons Stevia Extract Powder
- 2 teaspoons unbleached white flour
- 2 teaspoons cornstarch or arrowroot powder
- 1/4 teaspoon Stevia Extract Powder
- Clean kitchen towel for turning out cake
- Suggestions for filling: Blueberry Jam, Lemon Pudding, 1 cup sliced strawberries in Whipped Cream (see index)

Line an 11 x 15 inch jelly roll pan with waxed paper. Lightly oil paper or spray with non-stick coating.

In medium mixing bowl beat egg whites until stiff peaks form; set aside. Beat yolks and water in small mixing bowl to a thick, lemon colored stage, adding vanilla as it thickens. Stir together the baking powder, flour, and stevia. Slowly add to the yolk mixture while folding carefully with a rubber spatula. Fold in beaten egg whites. Spread cake batter in prepared pan. Bake at 360 degrees in a preheated oven for 11 or 12 minutes to a golden color.

While cake bakes stir flour, cornstarch, and stevia together; place in a mesh tea strainer. In an area 11 x 15 inches sift mixture over towel by tapping strainer with a spoon. Turn out cake and remove waxed paper. Immediately roll cake "jelly roll" fashion starting with the shorter side and including towel. Cool on rack. Unroll and spread with filling. Re-roll and cover with plastic wrap. Refrigerate until serving time.

This cake is best when served 1 to 5 hours after preparation, but leftovers are quite all right the following day. Optional: Fresh fruit pieces or mint leaves make a nice garnish.

Berry Citrus Pudding Cake

Yields 6 servings

This delectable sponge cake forms its own sauce.

- 5 tablespoons barley flour OR whole wheat pastry flour
- 1 teaspoon Stevia Extract Powder
- dash nutmeg
- 1/8 teaspoon salt
- 1 cup yogurt
- 1/4 teaspoon dry lemon peel
- 1/4 cup freshly squeezed lemon juice
- few drops lemon extract
- 2 tablespoons vegetable oil
- 1/4 cup coconut meal
- 2 large egg yolks
- 3 large egg whites at room temperature
- 1 1/2 cups fresh or frozen blackberries
- 1/2 teaspoon Powdered Stevia Garnish (see index)

In a medium bowl stir together flour, stevia, nutmeg, and salt. Use a separate bowl to mix yogurt, lemon peel, juice, lemon extract, oil, coconut meal, and egg yolks. Combine these 2 mixtures.

Beat egg whites until stiff peaks form. Fold into the cake batter. Next fold in the blackberries. Turn into a lightly oiled 8 inch square baking dish. Bake in a preheated 350 degree oven for 20 minutes. Lower heat to 325 degrees and bake an additional 15 minutes.

Remove from oven. Place powdered garnish in a tea strainer and sprinkle over cake. Serve warm.

Buttercream Frosting Yields about 1 3/4 cups frosting

This amount generously covers a 2 layer cake.

- 3 tablespoons cornstarch or arrowroot powder
- 2 tablespoons nonfat dry milk or 1 tablespoon rice beverage powder
- 3/4 teaspoon Stevia Extract Powder
- 1 cup water (or 3/4 cup when using tofu)
- 1/4 cup butter, softened
- 4 ounces cream cheese, softened, or 4 ounces soft silken style tofu
- 2 teaspoons vanilla extract
- few drops lemon extract

In a small saucepan stir together cornstarch, dry milk, stevia, and water. Cook over medium heat, stirring constantly, until quite thick. Cool to room temperature.

Place remaining ingredients in a deep bowl. Beat for 2 minutes. Add the cornstarch mixture and beat another 2 minutes. If necessary, chill before spreading.

Variations:

- Spiced Frosting – beat in 1/4 teaspoon cinnamon and a shake of nutmeg.

- Coconut Frosting – sprinkle on 1/2 cup unsulphured, toasted coconut.

- Almond Frosting – Omit vanilla extract. Add 1/2 to 3/4 teaspoon almond extract and sprinkle with 1/2 cup blanched, sliced almonds.

- Lemon Frosting – Omit dry milk. Increase stevia to 1 1/4 teaspoons. Reduce water to 3/4 cup and add 1/4 cup fresh lemon juice. Reduce vanilla to 1/4 teaspoon.

Vanilla Yogurt Frosting

Covers a 2 layer cake

This versatile frosting is creamy and delicious.

- 1/2 cup plain low fat yogurt
- 1 package (8 ounces) Neufchatel cheese, softened
- 3/4 teaspoon Stevia Extract Powder
- 1 1/2 teaspoons vanilla extract

Place all ingredients in a small, deep mixing bowl and beat until smooth. Chill. Spread on cake. In warm weather, refrigerate leftovers.

Tip: Add nonfat dry milk for thicker frosting or water to thin.

Variations:
- Carob powder (1 or 2 tablespoons) can be added as well as chopped walnuts or pecans.

- Sprinkle top of cake with toasted, unsweetened coconut.

- Decorate with whole pecans or sliced almonds.

Chapter 12
Delectable Desserts

Most puddings can be prepared well in advance, making them ideal for serving company. Holiday Bread Pudding, though, needs to be served warm. This "grand" version of country style fare uses an unlikely combination of spicy ingredients.

Fruit Pudding is also out of the ordinary. It's fast and easy to prepare and boasts an impressive flavor. Low fat cottage cheese and yogurt add richness.

These desserts can easily be doubled in order to have some left over to serve the next day. Cover carefully and keep refrigerated. Add garnish just before serving.

Lite Peach Mousse

This tasty crowd-pleaser can be prepared well ahead of serving.

- 1/2 cup white grape juice
- 4 cups sliced fresh peaches OR 5 cups frozen peach slices
- 1/2 teaspoon Stevia Extract Powder
- 1/4 cup cornstarch OR arrowroot powder
- 1/2 cup white grape juice
- juice of one small lemon
- 1/2 teaspoon almond extract
- 1 recipe Fluffy Vanilla Whip (see index)
- fresh berries and mint leaves for garnish, optional

Bring to a boil 1/2 cup white grape juice and the peaches in a medium saucepan. Reduce heat and simmer, stirring as needed. As peaches soften, cut into smaller pieces with a batter beater or mash slightly.

Mix stevia, cornstarch, and 1/2 cup white grape juice in a cup. Stir into simmering peaches and cook until thickened. Remove from heat and stir in lemon juice and almond extract. Cool to room temperature.

Prepare Fluffy Vanilla Whip. Fold into the peach mixture and spoon into a decorative serving bowl. Cover and refrigerate. Garnish.

Tip: This mousse can be used to fill a 9 or 10 inch baked pie shell.

Festive Dessert Squares

Yields 12 servings

Luscious layers of kiwi fruit, pineapple, and cheese filling over a crunchy crust.

- 1 cup whole wheat pastry flour
- 1 tablespoon toasted wheat germ
- 1/4 cup finely chopped pecans
- 1/3 cup butter, softened
- 1 package (8 ounce) Neufchatel cheese
- 3/4 teaspoon Stevia Extract Powder
- 2 eggs
- 2 tablespoons toasted wheat germ
- 3/4 cup soft tofu (½ of a 12 ounce package)
- 3/4 cup pineapple juice OR 1 (6 ounce) can
- 2 tablespoons cornstarch OR arrowroot powder
- 1/4 teaspoon Stevia Extract Powder
- 1 can (20 ounces) crushed pineapple OR 1 1/4 cups cooked pineapple in 1 cup juice
- 1/2 cup whipping cream OR 1 cup Fluffy Vanilla Whip (see index)
- 4 kiwi fruit, peeled and sliced

Mix first 4 ingredients in an 8 inch square baking dish and press on the bottom for crust. Bake at 350 degrees in a preheated oven for 20 minutes.

Process cheese, 3/4 teaspoon stevia, eggs, 2 tablespoons wheat germ, tofu, and pineapple juice in blender bowl until smooth. Pour over hot crust. Bake at 350 degrees for 25 minutes. Cool.

In a saucepan combine cornstarch, 1/4 teaspoon stevia, and pineapple in juice. Cook and stir over medium heat until thickened. Cool.

Whip cream in a small, deep bowl. Fold into pineapple mixture and spread over cheese layer. Refrigerate 3 hours or longer. Serve topped with kiwi fruit.

Steamed Pears in Raspberry Syrup
Yields 6 Servings

Nectar-sweet raspberry syrup over tender pears.

- 6 large ripe pears, such as Bartlett
- 1½ cups natural white grape-raspberry juice blend
- 2 tablespoons cornstarch OR arrowroot powder
- ¼ cup cold water
- ½ teaspoon Stevia Extract Powder
- fresh raspberries or mint leaves for garnish

Leave pears whole. Peel and remove cores with a melon baller or small measuring spoon. Set upright in a saucepan and add the fruit juice. Cover and simmer about 20 minutes. Remove pears to a serving dish.

Combine cornstarch, water, and stevia. Add to the liquid in the saucepan and simmer just to thicken. Pour syrup over pears. Serve warm or chilled. Garnish.

Variation: Top with a dollop of Cottage Sour Cream or Whipped Cream (see index).

Vanilla Poached Pears

Yields 6 servings

Vanilla combines nicely with the light pear flavor.

- 3/4 cup water
- 1/2 teaspoon Stevia Extract Powder
- 1/2 teaspoon vanilla extract
- 3 large ripe pears such as Bartlett
- 1 tablespoon cornstarch OR arrowroot powder
- 1/4 cup water
- 2 tablespoons fruit jam or spread
- fresh stevia or mint leaves for garnish, optional

Measure 3/4 cup water, stevia, and vanilla extract into a medium saucepan.

Halve and peel pears. Remove seed core with a melon baller or teaspoon tip. Trim blossom end. Place pears in the stevia mixture and bring to a boil. Reduce heat and simmer 15 minutes.

Lift pears to a serving dish. Dissolve cornstarch in the 1/4 cup water and stir into remaining liquid in the saucepan. Stir and simmer to thicken. Spoon over pears. Chill.

To serve, top each pear piece with a teaspoon of jam and garnish as desired.

Variation: Sprinkle with nutmeg, coriander, ginger, or cinnamon.

Pineapple Grape Ambrosia

Yields 6 servings

Here's a scrumptious light dessert, a supper favorite.

- 1 3/4 cups cooked pineapple chunks with juice OR 1 (20 ounce) can pineapple chunks
- 1/4 teaspoon Stevia Extract Powder
- 2 tablespoons cornstarch OR arrowroot powder
- 1 teaspoon vanilla extract
- 2 tablespoons chopped almonds or walnuts
- 2 tablespoons unsulphured coconut, shredded
- 3/4 cup cooked brown rice, cooled
- 1/2 cup purple grapes, halved and seeded
- 1/2 recipe Cottage Sour Cream (see index)

Drain pineapple, reserving juice. Add water to equal 1 cup. Measure stevia, cornstarch, juice, and vanilla extract into a medium saucepan. Bring to a boil, reduce heat, and simmer a minute to thicken sauce, stirring as needed.

Cool to room temperature. Fold in pineapple chunks, almonds, coconut, rice, and grapes. Cover and chill. Top servings with a dollop of Cottage Sour Cream.

Variation: Reduce vanilla extract to 1/2 teaspoon and add grated fresh ginger to taste.

Hot Peaches 'N Cream

Easy to prepare, heavenly to eat! No "real" cream here.

- 3 tablespoons orange juice
- ½ teaspoon Stevia Extract Powder
- ¼ teaspoon coriander
- 2 cups sliced, fresh peaches OR 3 cups frozen sliced peaches, thawed
- 3 tablespoons orange juice
- 2 teaspoons cornstarch OR arrowroot powder
- plain lowfat yogurt OR Cottage Sour Cream (see index)

Combine 3 tablespoons orange juice, stevia, and coriander in a medium saucepan. Stir and add peaches. Bring to a boil over medium heat, then reduce to a simmer. Cook 3 minutes, stirring as needed.

Dissolve cornstarch in remaining 3 tablespoons orange juice. Add to simmering peaches, cook and stir to thicken. Serve hot, topped with a generous dollop of yogurt or "cream."

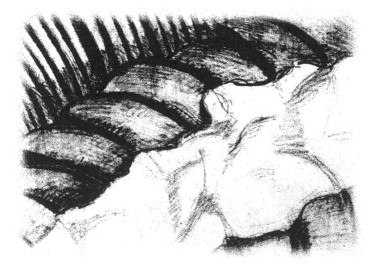

Carob Cream Pudding

Enjoy this rich, dark, delectable dessert.

- 2 tablespoons carob powder
- 1 teaspoon Stevia Extract Powder
- 5 tablespoons cornstarch or arrowroot powder
- 2 cups milk
- 1 cup water
- 2 eggs
- 2 teaspoons vanilla extract
- 1 tablespoon butter

Combine carob powder, stevia, and cornstarch in a double boiler pan. Gradually stir in milk and water. Place over boiling water and stir while mixture thickens.

Lightly beat eggs and dip about 1/2 cup pudding into the eggs. Combine well and then add back to the pudding as it cooks. Reduce heat to low and continue cooking another 3 minutes. Remove from heat.

Stir vanilla extract and butter into pudding. Serve warm or chilled.

Variation:
- Top with a few slices of banana and a sprinkling of Oat Cinnamon Crunch (see index) just before serving.

- For chocolate pudding, substitue 2 tablespoons cocoa powder for the carob powder and increase Stevia Extract Powder to 1 1/2 **teaspoons.**

Non Dairy Carob Cream Pudding
Yields 6 servings

This yummy pudding contains no eggs or dairy milk.

2 tablespoons carob powder
1 teaspoon Stevia Extract Powder
6 tablespoons cornstarch or arrowroot powder
2 cups soymilk
1 cup water
2 teaspoons vanilla extract
1 tablespoon nutbutter such as cashew or peanut (optional)

Combine carob powder, stevia, and cornstarch in a double boiler pan. Gradually stir in soymilk and water. Place over boiling water and stir as mixture thickens. Reduce heat to low and continue cooking another minute. Remove from heat. Stir in vanilla and nutbutter, if used. Serve warm or chilled.

Variation: Top with banana slices and a sprinkle of nuts.

Tip:
- This recipe illustrates how a pudding can be converted to dairy-free.
- Add a dash of salt if you like.

Fruit Pudding

Yields 6 servings

Cherries and pineapple chunks hidden in a "snowy" pudding.

- 1 cup low fat cottage cheese
- 1/4 teaspoon almond extract
- 1 teaspoon vanilla extract
- 1/4 teaspoon dry lemon peel
- 1/2 teaspoon Stevia Extract Powder
- 3/4 cup plain low fat yogurt
- 1 can (12 ounce) unsweetened pineapple chunks OR 1 cup fresh pineapple chunks
- 1 cup frozen dark sweet cherries, thawed OR 1 cup fresh cherries
- 1/2 cup chopped walnuts, toasted or raw

In a blender bowl, whiz cottage cheese until smooth. This takes only a few seconds. Add almond and vanilla extracts, dry lemon peel, stevia, and yogurt. Blend again just until mixed. Refrigerate.

Drain pineapple chunks and reserve juice for another use. Spoon equal amounts of fruit into each of 6 dessert dishes. Cover with the cheese mixture and a sprinkle of nuts.

Serve immediately.

Variation: Oat Cinnamon Crunch (see index) can be used in place of walnuts.

Basic Tapioca Pudding   Yields 5 or 6 servings

An old favorite with some new variations

- 3 tablespoons minute tapioca
- 2 1/4 cups skim milk
- 1 egg, lightly beaten
- A dash of salt
- 1/2 cup plain low fat yogurt
- 1/2 teaspoon Stevia Extract Powder
- 1 1/4 teaspoons vanilla extract
- 1/4 cup finely chopped walnuts (optional)

Combine tapioca and milk in a medium saucepan. Set aside 5 minutes to soften. Thoroughly whip in egg and salt. Over moderate heat bring to a boil, stirring constantly. Remove from heat and cool 15 minutes.

Mix together yogurt, stevia, and vanilla; stir into tapioca. It's delicious warm or chilled. Sprinkle with nuts if desired.

Variations:
- Soy milk can be used in place of dairy milk.
- Omit nuts; top pudding with 1 or 2 of the following (see index):
  Oat Cinnamon Crunch
  Strawberry Spread
  Apple Grape Jam
  sliced bananas or other fruit (add just before serving)
- Fold in chopped fruit.

Holiday Bread Pudding
Yields 10 servings

An elegant version of a usually humble dessert.

- 6 cups lightly toasted whole wheat bread cubes
- 1 cup sugarfree frozen cherry juice concentrate (or cherry combination)*
- 1 2/3 cups water
- 1 teaspoon Stevia Extract Powder
- 1 cup frozen cranberries
- 1 1/4 teaspoon cinnamon
- 1/4 teaspoon nutmeg
- 1 cup chopped, unsulphured prunes
- 1/3 cup butter

Be sure to toast the bread first. It goes quickly in a regular toaster.

Lightly oil a 2 quart casserole and add bread cubes. In a large saucepan combine juice, water, and stevia. Stir to dissolve. Add cranberries, spices, and prunes. Reserve 2 tablespoons of butter and add the rest to the saucepan. Bring to a boil and cook gently until the cranberries soften (about 7 minutes).

Pour cranberry mixture over the bread in the casserole. Set aside for 10 minutes. Heat oven to 350 degrees. Dot top of pudding with reserved butter and bake about 45 minutes. Serve warm. Refrigerate leftovers and reheat to serve.

Variations:

- Other sugarfree red fruit juice concentrates can be used in place of cherry.
- Vary the amounts of water and bread cubes for a firmer or softer pudding.
- Delicious as is or top with ice cream (see index).

* Black cherry juice concentrate from a health food store can be used. Follow label instructions, mixing it double strength. Add ¼ teaspoon Stevia Extract Powder.

Lemon Pudding

Creamy smooth with a rich lemon flavor.

- 1/4 cup cornstarch or arrowroot powder
- 3/4 teaspoons Stevia Extract Powder
- 1/8 teaspoon salt (optional)
- 2 1/4 cups skim milk
- 1 whole egg
- 1 egg white
- 1 teaspoon vanilla extract
- 1 teaspoon lemon extract
- 2 tablespoons butter

In a medium saucepan dissolve cornstarch, stevia, and salt in the milk. Slightly beat the egg and egg white and stir into the milk mixture. Place over medium heat. Bring to a boil and then simmer for 5 minutes, stirring constantly. Remove from heat and stir in extracts and butter.

Cool to room temperature and refrigerate before serving.

Variations:
- Salt can be omitted.
- Use soymilk in place of dairy milk. For a softer pudding, increase milk to 2 1/2 cups.

Cream Puffs

Tender, golden puffs with your choice of filling.

- 1 cup water
- A pinch of Stevia Extract Powder
- 1/2 cup butter
- 1 cup whole wheat pastry flour
- 4 eggs

Combine water, stevia, and butter in a medium saucepan and bring to a boil. Add flour all at once while stirring vigorously with a mixing spoon. Cook, stirring until mixture pulls from the sides of the pan. Remove from heat. Cool about 12 minutes.

Beat with a spoon while adding eggs, one at a time. Continue beating until smooth. Spoon batter by heaping tablespoons 3 or 4 inches apart on a greased baking sheet. Bake in a preheated oven at 360 degrees for about 35 minutes or until golden. Cool on racks.

Split and fill with any of the following (see index):

Whipped Cream
Lemon Pudding
Cherry Sauce

Serve or cover and refrigerate until serving time.

Apple Nut Crisp

Yields 7 servings

This is a traditional Missouri dessert for a family meal.

- 5 cups sliced apples
- 1/4 cup natural apple juice
- A dash of nutmeg
- 1/2 teaspoon cinnamon
- 1/2 cup barley flour
- 1/4 teaspoon Stevia Extract Powder
- 1/2 teaspoon cinnamon
- 1/2 cup plus 2 tablespoons rolled oats, lightly chopped in a blender.
- 6 tablespoons vegetable oil
- 1/4 to 1/2 cup chopped walnuts or pecans
- 1/4 cup unsweetened coconut meal

Apples need not be peeled if they are organic. In a lightly oiled 8 x 8 inch baking dish place apples, then sprinkle with juice, nutmeg, and 1/2 teaspoon cinnamon. Stir. In a bowl mix together flour, stevia, 1/2 teaspoon cinnamon, and oats. Stir in oil, walnuts, and coconut meal. Spoon over apple mixture. Bake at 350 degrees in a preheated oven for 50 minutes or until apples are tender, To prevent over-browning, loosely cover with aluminum foil the last 15 minutes.

Serve warm or chilled. For special events top with Lemon Ice Cream (see index).

Variation:
Substitute whole wheat pastry flour for barley flour.

Fresh Peach Crunch

Mellow sliced peaches are a nice contrast to the spicy crunch.

- 1/2 cup whole wheat flour
- 1/4 teaspoon Stevia Extract Powder OR 3/4 teaspoon Green Stevia Powder
- 1/4 teaspoon cinnamon
- dash of cloves or allspice
- 1/3 cup rolled oats
- 1/4 cup walnuts, chopped
- 3 tablespoons vegetable oil
- 4 peaches, peeled and sliced
- 2 tablespoons fresh lemon juice
- 1 tablespoon water
- 1/4 teaspoon Stevia Extract Powder
- 1 recipe of either Whipped Cream or Pineapple Sauce (see index)

Stir together flour, stevia, salt, and spices in a small bowl. Add oats and walnuts. Mix. Sprinkle with oil and stir in. Press into a lightly oiled 8 inch square pan and bake about 10 minutes or until lightly browned in a 350 degree oven. Cool and break into chunks.

Peel and slice peaches into a small bowl. Dissolve stevia in lemon juice combined with water. Sprinkle over peaches and stir.

Layer peaches and crunch in 5 dessert bowls or parfait glasses. Top as desired. Refrigerate until serving time.

Variation: Barley flour or whole wheat pastry flour can replace whole wheat flour.

Dessert Crepes

Crepes are an easy way to add elegance to any meal.

Crepes:
- 3/4 cup plus 2 tablespoons whole wheat pastry flour
- 1 1/2 cups water
- 1/4 cup nonfat dry milk OR 3 tablespoons rice beverage powder
- 3 eggs
- 1 tablespoon vegetable oil
- 1/8 teaspoon Stevia Extract Powder
- 1/8 teaspoon salt

Suggested fillings:
- Strawberries prepared as for strawberry shortcake
- Sliced bananas in Whipped Cream or Fruit Pudding (see index)

Suggested toppings:
- Cherry Sauce, Very Orange Sauce, or Pineapple Sauce (see index)

Stir all crepe ingredients together to completely blend. Refrigerate batter for 1 hour.

Preheat a heavy skillet over moderate heat. The heat can be adjusted as crepes cook. Lightly oil the skillet. Use 2 tablespoons of batter per crepe and quickly swirl with the back of a spoon to a 6 inch circle. Cook about 1 minute. Turn and continue cooking about 1/2 minute longer. Remove to a plate to cool. Crepes can be stacked.

Place about 1/3 cup filling down the middle of each crepe and roll. Place on dessert dishes. Serve immediately, topped with sauce, or refrigerate and pour sauce just before serving.

Tip: Crepes may be frozen 4 to 6 weeks. Place waxed paper between crepes. To use, thaw at room temperature 1 hour.

Peach and Apricot Gel

A delectable, easy dessert for a crowd.

- 1 can (16 ounce) sugarfree apricot halves OR 2 cups fresh apricot halves cooked in 1/2 cup water
- 1 can (16 ounce) sugarfree sliced peaches OR 2 cups fresh peach halves cooked in 1/2 cup water
- 2 envelopes unflavored gelatin OR 4 tablespoons agar agar
- Natural apple juice as needed
- 1/4 teaspoon Stevia Extract Powder OR 3/4 teaspoon Green Stevia Powder
- 1/8 teaspoon cinnamon
- few drops of almond extract
- 1/2 recipe Vanilla Yogurt Frosting (see index)
- 1/2 cup toasted, unsulphured, shredded coconut

Drain peaches and apricots into a large measuring cup. Add apple juice to equal 3 1/2 cups liquid. Measure 1 cup of this juice into a small saucepan. Sprinkle gelatin over the surface and set aside to soften for 5 minutes. Place over low heat and stir to dissolve gelatin. For agar agar, sprinkle over 3 cups juice, bring to a boil, then simmer 5 minutes.

Stir stevia, cinnamon, and almond extract into the remaining juice. Combine with gelatin or agar agar mixture. Cut each apricot half into 4 pieces. Turn fruit into an 8 X 12 inch baking dish or large fruit bowl. Pour prepared gelatin mixture over fruit. Chill.

When firm, spread with Vanilla Yogurt Frosting (see index) and sprinkle coconut over all. Cover and refrigerate until serving time.

Variation:
Substitute Oat Cinnamon Crunch (see index) for coconut.

Pumpkin Chiffon Squares   Yields 8 or 9 servings

Make this one in advance. It tastes best the second day.

- 3/4 cup rice flour OR whole wheat Pastry Flour
- 1/4 cup butter
- 1/4 cup finely chopped walnuts
- 1/2 cup skim milk
- 1 egg
- 1/4 teaspoon cinnamon
- shake each of ginger and nutmeg
- 1 envelope unflavored gelatin OR 2 tablespoons agar agar
- 1/2 teaspoon Stevia Extract Powder
- 1 cup solid packed pumpkin OR 1 cup steamed, home-cooked pumpkin.
- 4 ounces Neufchatel cheese
- 1/2 teaspoon Stevia Extract Powder
- 1/4 cup milk
- 1 teaspoon each vanilla extract & butterscotch flavoring
- 1/2 cup whipping cream, whipped
- 1/2 cup Oat Cinnamon Crunch (see index)

Mix together flour, butter, and walnuts in an 8 inch square baking dish. Press down firmly to form a crust (bottom of dish only). Bake at 350 degrees in a preheated oven for 15 minutes or until lightly browned.

In a medium saucepan stir together 1/2 cup milk, egg, and spices. Sprinkle gelatin or agar agar over surface and set aside to soften for 5 minutes. Place over medium heat and stir while bringing to a boil. Continue to stir and cook over low heat for 5 minutes. Remove from heat and stir in 1/2 teaspoon stevia until completely dissolved. Stir in pumpkin. Chill until mixture mounds slightly when stirred.

In a small, deep mixing bowl beat together Neufchatel cheese, 1/2 teaspoon stevia, 1/4 cup milk, vanilla extract, and butterscotch flavoring. Fold into pumpkin mixture. Fold in whipped cream and spoon over baked crust. Top with Oat Cinnamon Crunch. Cover with plastic wrap and chill overnight.

133

Rosanna's Baked Cheesecake   Yields a 9 inch cake

Rich, delicious cheesecake with a vegetarian soy version.

- 1 recipe Easy Oil Pastry (see index)
- 1/2 teaspoon cinnamon
- 1 package (8 ounce) cream cheese, softened
- 1 carton (8 ounce) sour cream
- 1 teaspoon Stevia Extract Powder
- 1 tablespoon whole wheat pastry flour
- 2 teaspoons vanilla
- 1 teaspoon dry lemon peel
- 1 egg
- 1 cup plain low fat yogurt

Mix Pastry in a 9 inch pie dish, adding the cinnamon to the dry ingredients. Press into the pie dish. Bake 6 minutes only and remove from oven.

Combine cream cheese, sour cream, stevia, flour, vanilla, and lemon peel. Beat until fluffy. Add egg and yogurt, then beat on low speed until combined.

Pour batter into partially baked crust. Bake in a 350 degree preheated oven about 45 to 55 minutes. Filling should be set, but a bit soft in the very center. Cool completely, cover, and refrigerate. Best served the following day.

Serve with Cherry Sauce (see index) or other fruit sauce.

For a soy version, make the following changes:

Omit cream cheese, sour cream, yogurt, and 1 tablespoon flour.

Add 12 ounces soft, silken style tofu, 8 ounces plain soy yogurt, 2 tablespoons cornstarch, and ¼ cup non-hydrogenated margarine. Increase eggs to 2.

Mix as above.

Royal Clyde Cheesecake   Yields 9 servings

A classic no-bake cheesecake and fresh strawberry topping.

- 1 recipe Crisp Cookie Crust (see index), baked
- 1/2 cup whipping cream
- 8 ounces Neufchatel cheese, softened
- 3/4 cup cold water
- 1 teaspoon Stevia Extract Powder
- 2 tablespoons agar agar or 1 envelope unflavored gelatin
- 1/2 cup milk
- 1/4 cup fresh lemon juice
- 1/2 cup plain yogurt
- 1/4 teaspoon Stevia Extract Powder
- 1 tablespoon water
- 2 pints fresh strawberries, hulled and sliced

Cool the baked crust. Whip the cream in a small, deep bowl. Refrigerate. Beat cheese in a medium bowl until fluffy and set aside.

Measure 3/4 cup water and stevia into a small saucepan. Sprinkle agar agar (or gelatin) on top and set aside to soften 5 minues. Bring to a boil and then simmer 5 minutes (or for gelatin, melt over low heat). Cool just to room temperature – do not let it firm up. Beat into the fluffy cheese until well mixed. Add milk, lemon juice, and yogurt. Cool until slightly thickened. Carefully fold in whipped cream. Spoon. Spoon into crust and chill several hours.

Dissolve 1/4 teaspoon stevia in 1 tablespoon water and stir into strawberries. Serve over cheesecake.

Variations:
- Alternate toppings are Peach Jam, Cranberry Applesauce, or Very Orange Sauce (see index for all of these).
- Easy Oil Pastry (see index) also works well with this cheesecake.

Peach Cobbler

Yields 6 to 8 servings

Featuring sweet peaches under crumbly, golden topping.

- 3/4 teaspoon Stevia Extract Powder
- 2 eggs
- 2 tablespoons whole wheat pastry flour
- 1/2 teaspoon cinnamon
- dash of nutmeg
- 4 cups peeled, sliced fresh peaches (about 5)
- 3/4 cup whole wheat pastry flour
- 1/8 teaspoon Stevia Extract Powder
- 1/2 teaspoon baking powder
- 1/4 teaspoon salt (optional)
- 3 tablespoons butter, softened
- 1 egg
- 1 1/2 tablespoons water
- 1 teaspoon cornstarch
- 1/8 teaspoon Stevia Extract Powder
- 1/4 teaspoon cinnamon

In a large bowl stir together stevia, eggs, flour, cinnamon, and nutmeg. Mix in peaches. Pour into a lightly oiled, 7 x 11 inch baking dish.

In another bowl stir together flour, stevia, baking powder, and salt. Cut in butter until crumbly. Stir in egg and water until moistened only. Crumble over peaches.

Mix cornstarch, stevia, and cinnamon. Place in a mesh tea strainer and sift over cobbler. Bake in a preheated 350 degree oven for 50 to 55 minutes. Cover loosely with aluminum foil the last 15 minutes, if necessary, to avoid over-browning. Serve warm or at room temperature. If desired, top with Whipped Cream, Pineapple Sauce (warm), or Very Orange Sauce (see index).

Fresh Fruit Compote   Yields 5 servings

Sweet and sassy blend of flavors for breakfast or dessert.

- Juice squeezed from 1 orange plus water to make 1/2 cup.
- 1/2 tablespoon fresh lime or lemon juice
- 1/2 teaspoon Stevia Extract Powder
- 1/4 teaspoon Ginger Tea Concentrate (see index) or sprinkle ground ginger on each serving
- 2 pears, cut in large chunks
- 3 ripe kiwi fruit, thickly sliced
- fresh berries for topping
- fresh mint leaves for garnish (optional)

Place orange juice, lemon juice, stevia, and Ginger Tea Concentrate in a bowl. Stir to dissolve stevia. Add pears and kiwi fruit, then stir gently. Refrigerate 1 to 3 hours, stirring once each hour.

Divide among 5 dessert dishes. Add topping and garnish.

Variations:
- 1 1/2 cups fresh pineapple chunks can replace kiwi fruit.
- Omit berry topping and sprinkle with cinnamon.

Pear Pineapple Compote

A lightly spiced fruit blend.

- 1 can (20 ounce) sugarfree pineapple chunks OR 2 cups fresh pineapple chunks cooked in ½ cup water
- 1 can (16 ounce) sugarfree sliced pears OR 1 ⅔ cups fresh sliced pears cooked in ⅓ cup water
- 1 tablespoon cornstarch or arrowroot powder
- 1/8 teaspoon ground allspice
- ¼ teaspoon Stevia Extract Powder
- 2 teaspoons fresh lemon juice
- 1 cup (8 ounce carton) plain low fat yogurt
- ¼ teaspoon Stevia Extract Powder
- few drops lemon extract
- chopped fresh mint or lemon twist for garnish (optional)

     Drain juice from fruit into medium saucepan. Blend in the cornstarch and allspice. Cook and stir until bubbly. Remove from heat and stir in ¼ teaspoon stevia and lemon juice. Gently combine with fruit. Chill. Spoon into dessert dishes.

     With a whisk combine yogurt, ¼ teaspoon stevia, and lemon extract. Spoon over fruit and serve.

Variation: Use apricot halves instead of pears.

Chapter 13

All-American Pies

Now stevia can sweeten your favorite pie! Follow the meringue instructions as stated. Do not beat stevia into the egg whites as it may deflate the meringue. There is plenty of sweetness in the filling and topping.

For the "Punkin Center Pie," begin with the recipe given and then experiment with your own combination of spices. Every region has its own ideas about spicing a pumpkin pie.

Sometimes aluminum foil is needed toward the end to prevent over-browning of the crust while the filling cooks.

Be sure to refrigerate leftovers. For those preferring warm pie, re-heating is easy and quick in a toaster oven or electric skillet. "As American as Apple Pie?" Yes, indeed!

Lemon Cream Pie

Yields a 9 inch pie

Topped with exquisite fruit glaze.

- Pastry for a 9 inch crust sweetened with 1/4 teaspoon Stevia Extract Powder, baked
- 1/4 cup cornstarch OR arrowroot powder
- 1 1/4 teaspoon Stevia Extract Powder
- 1/8 teaspoon salt
- 1 cup plus 2 tablespoons milk OR soymilk
- 1/4 cup water
- 3 egg yolks
- 1/3 cup fresh lemon juice
- 1 teaspoon grated lemon peel
- 1/2 cup plain yogurt
- 2 tablespoons butter
- 3/4 cup white grape juice
- 1/8 teaspoon Stevia Extract Powder
- 1 tablespoon cornstarch OR arrowroot powder
- kiwi fruit wedges or strawberry halves

Stir cornstarch, 1 1/4 teaspoon stevia, salt, milk, water, and egg yolks in a medium saucepan. Place over medium heat and bring to a boil while stirring. Reduce heat and simmer 3 minutes. Remove from heat and stir in lemon juice, peel, yogurt, and butter. Turn into baked crust. Cool and refrigerate.

For glaze, stir grape juice, 1/8 teaspoon stevia, and cornstarch in a small saucepan. Stir and cook over medium heat to thicken. Cool to room temperature.

Arrange fruit pieces atop pie. Pour glaze over fruit. Chill 4 hours.

Variation: 1/4 cup sour cream can replace half of the yogurt.

Jubilee Orange Pie

Yields an 8 inch pie

Enjoy a burst of citrus with this tofu-based pie.

- Pastry for an 8 inch crust
- 1 package (12 ounce) silken style firm tofu
- 2 1/2 teaspoons grated lemon peel
- 1/4 teaspoon vanilla extract
- 1 1/8 teaspoon Stevia Extract Powder
- 1/3 cup plain yogurt or soy yogurt
- 1/3 cup frozen orange juice concentrate
- 2 tablespoons butter
- 1/3 cup thick, natural applesauce
- fresh kiwi fruit slices or hulled strawberries

Preheat oven to 350 degrees and pre-bake pastry 9 minutes only.

Combine the next 8 ingredients in a blender bowl and process until smooth. Pour into pre-baked shell and bake 25 to 30 minutes at 350 degrees. Filling will not be firm in the center, but will solidify as it chills. Cool, then refrigerate several hours.

Serve pie wedges topped with fruit pieces.

Variation: For a meringue-like topping, omit fresh fruit. Spread pie with Fluffy Vanilla Whip (see index) and sprinkle with toasted, unsulphured coconut.

Chilled Apple Pie

Yields a 10 inch pie

Spicy apple pie with a Fluffy Vanilla Whip layer.

- 1 1/2 cups apple juice.
- 2 tablespoons cornstarch
- 1/2 teaspoon coriander
- 1/2 teaspoon cinnamon
- 1/4 teaspoon cardamom
- 1 teaspoon Stevia Extract Powder
- 3 tablespoons butter
- 6 Jonathan apples, peeled, cored, sliced (about 7 cups)
- Pastry for a 10 inch crust, baked
- 1 recipe Fluffy Vanilla Whip with 1/8 teaspoon cinnamon added

Combine the first 6 ingredients in a medium saucepan. Cook and stir over medium heat to thicken. Set aside.

Melt butter in a Dutch oven and stir in apples. Cook and stir over medium low heat until apples are tender and slightly browned, about 10 minutes. Stir into sauce and turn into pie crust. Refrigerate.

Prepare Fluffy Vanilla Whip, adding cinnamon along with stevia. Spread over top of cooled pie.

Strawberry Cheese Pie

Yields a 9 inch pie

No need to beat cream separately for this scrumptious pie.

- Pastry for a 9 inch crust, baked
- 3/4 cup white grape juice
- 2 tablespoons cornstarch OR arrowroot powder
- 1/2 teaspoon Stevia Extract Powder
- 1 quart (1 1/4 pounds) strawberries, hulled
- 4 ounces cream cheese OR soy cream cheese
- 1/4 teaspoon Stevia Extract Powder
- 1/2 teaspoon orange extract
- 1/2 cup whipping cream
- 2 tablespoons milk

For glaze combine juice, cornstarch, and 1/2 teaspoon stevia in a medium saucepan. Slice 1 1/2 cup of the strawberries and add to the saucepan. Cook and stir over medium heat until mixture thickens. Mash berries if still lumpy.

Use a medium bowl to beat until fluffy the cream cheese, 1/4 teaspoon stevia, orange extract, whipping cream, and milk. Spoon into crust. Refrigerate.

Cut remaining strawberries in half or slice if they are large. Arrange over cheese layer. Spoon glaze over berries. Chill several hours before serving.

Punkin Center Pie

Yields a 10 inch pie

"Punkin Center" is a town in Nodaway County, Missouri.

- Pastry for a 10 inch pie, 1 crust
- 3/4 cup evaporated skim milk or 3/4 cup soymilk
- 1/3 teaspoon Stevia Extract Powder OR 1 teaspoon Green Stevia Powder
- 3 eggs
- 1 can (16 ounces) solid pack pumpkin OR 2 cups steamed and mashed pumpkin.
- 3/4 cup sugarfree, frozen apple juice concentrate OR simmer 1 cup natural apple juice to reduce to 3/4 cup.
- 1 1/4 teaspoons cinnamon
- 1/4 teaspoon nutmeg
- 1/8 teaspoons cloves
- Dash ginger or up to 1/4 teaspoon
- 1/4 teaspoon salt
- 2 tablespoons nonfat dry milk or soy beverage powder

Heat oven to 350 degrees. Fit pastry into a 10 inch pie dish and flute edges. Beat together evaporated milk, stevia, eggs, and pumpkin. Mix in remaining ingredients until well combined.

Pour filling into unbaked pie shell. Bake about 60 or 65 minutes or until a knife inserted near middle comes out clean. To prevent over-browning the crust edge, cover with strips of aluminum foil during the last 15 minutes of baking.

Cool on a wire rack. Cover and chill. This pie tastes best the second day. It can be topped with Whipped Cream (see index).

Tip: When using soymilk, increase soy beverage powder to 3 tablespoons.

Cherry Pie

Yields a 9 inch pie

A favorite for family celebrations.

- Pastry for a 2 crust pie
- 2 cans (16 ounce) water pack red tart cherries OR 4 cups fresh, tart, pitted cherries
- 1 1/4 teaspoons Stevia Extract Powder OR 4 teaspoons Green Stevia Powder.
- 1/8 teaspoon salt
- 3 tablespoons cornstarch
- 2 tablespoons butter
- 1/4 teaspoon almond extract
- 1 egg yolk beaten with 1 tablespoon water (optional)

Fit pastry for lower crust into pie dish. Reserve remaining pastry; cover and refrigerate.

Simmer fresh cherries in 1 1/2 cups water for 5 minutes. Drain cherries, reserving 1 cup juice. Combine stevia, salt, and cornstarch with cherry juice in a medium saucepan. Bring to a boil, stirring. Simmer 5 minutes. Stir in butter and almond extract. Carefully add cherries. Pour into prepared crust.

Dampen lower crust edges with water. Cut upper crust pastry into 1/2 inch strips. Arrange strips in lattice pattern atop the pie. Crimp edges together. There will be extra strips which can be baked for snacks. If desired, brush top pastry (not edges) with beaten egg yolk. Bake 35 minutes in 360 degree preheated oven, then reset oven to 325 degrees. Cover pie with aluminum foil to prevent over-browning. Bake another 15 minutes. Serve while still warm. Refrigerate leftovers. To serve, reheat gently.

Tip: Good with a scoop of Lemon Ice Cream (see index).

Elizabeth's Peach Pie

A perfect peach pie with a touch of spice.

- Pastry for a 2 crust pie
- 1 1/4 teaspoons Stevia Extract Powder
- 2 tablespoons cornstarch or arrowroot powder
- 1/4 teaspoon nutmeg
- 6 cups peeled, chopped peaches (3 pounds)
- 2 tablespoons fresh lemon juice
- 2 tablespoons butter

Preheat oven to 360 degrees. Combine stevia, cornstarch, and nutmeg. Add mixture to peaches and toss to coat. Let stand 5 minutes.

Place bottom crust in a 9 inch pie dish and cook for 5 minutes. Stir lemon juice in with the peaches, turn into pie dish, and dot with butter. Place top crust over peaches. Cut holes for steam. Place aluminum foil on the edges and set pan on cookie sheet. Bake for 25 minutes.

Remove foil and bake for another 35 minutes or until crust is golden.

Grandma's Apple Pie

Yields a 9 inch pie

A topping of Whipped Cream (see index) is a nice touch.

- Pastry for a 9 inch, 2 crust pie
- 6 cups peeled and thinly sliced pie apples such as Jonathan or Winesap.
- 1 or 2 teaspoons fresh lemon juice
- 1 1/2 teaspoons Stevia Extract Powder
- 2 to 3 tablespoons whole wheat pastry flour
- 1/4 teaspoon nutmeg
- 1 teaspoon cinnamon
- Dash of cloves or allspice
- 2 tablespoons butter

Fit bottom pastry into a pie dish. In a large mixing bowl sprinkle lemon juice over apples and stir to mix. Using a cup or small bowl stir together stevia, flour, nutmeg, cinnamon, and cloves or allspice. Sprinkle spice mixture over apples and carefully stir to coat apples. Pile apples into crust. Dot with butter.

With water, moisten the outer rim of the lower crust. Place upper crust on pie and crimp edges together. Slit top of pie to allow steam to escape. Place on a cookie sheet. Bake at 350 degrees in a preheated oven for 55 to 60 minutes. Aluminum foil can be placed over the pie during the last 15 minutes to prevent over-browning.

Cool on a rack, cover and leave at room temperature overnight or refrigerate if you like. This pie is delicious at any temperature.

Banana Cream Pie

Yields a 9 or 10 inch pie

Topped with golden meringue

- 9 or 10 inch baked pastry shell
- 1 teaspoon Stevia Extract Powder
- 5 tablespoons cornstarch
- 2 cups milk, soymilk, or rice milk.
- 1 cup water
- 4 eggs, separated
- 1 tablespoon butter
- 2 teaspoons vanilla extract
- few drops of lemon extract
- 1/4 teaspoon cream of tartar
- 1/2 teaspoon vanilla extract
- 3 medium ripe bananas
- 3 tablespoons unsweetened coconut meal

Place cornstarch and stevia in a double boiler pan. Gradually stir in milk and water. Place over boiling water and stir while mixture thickens.

Separate eggs. Reserve whites for meringue. Lightly stir the yolks. Dip about 1/2 cup pie filling into yolks and stir thoroughly. Add back to cooking pie filling. Reduce heat to low and continue cooking about 2 minutes. Remove from heat. Stir in butter, 2 teaspoons vanilla extract, and the lemon extract. Cool while preparing meringue.

In a bowl beat together egg whites, cream of tartar, and 1/2 teaspoon vanilla extract until stiff peaks form. Spread half the filling onto the crust. Slice bananas into the filling and spoon on remaining filling. Spread with meringue. Sprinkle coconut meal over meringue. Bake in a 350 degree preheated oven for 10 to 12 minutes or until golden.

Serve at room temperature and refrigerate leftovers.

Variation: An additional 1 cup of milk may replace the water.

Coconut Cream Pie
Yields a 9 or 10 inch pie

A rich coconut layer topped with fluffy meringue

- 9 or 10 inch baked pastry shell
- 1 teaspoon Stevia Extract Powder
- 5 tablespoons cornstarch
- 2 cups milk, soymilk, or rice milk
- 1 cup water
- 4 eggs, separated
- 2 tablespoons butter
- 2 teaspoons vanilla extract
- 1/4 teaspoon almond extract
- 1/4 teaspoon cream of tartar
- 1/2 teaspoon vanilla extract
- 3/4 cup unsulphured, shredded coconut
- 2 or 3 tablespoons coconut meal

Mix together stevia and cornstarch in a double boiler pan. Gradually stir in milk and water and place over boiling water. Stir while mixture thickens.

Separate eggs. Reserve whites for meringue. Lightly stir yolks. Dip about 1/2 cup pie filling into yolks and mix with a fork, then add back to the cooking pie filling and stir well. Turn heat to low and cook another 3 minutes. Remove from heat. Stir in butter, 2 teaspoons vanilla extract, and almond extract. Cool.

Prepare meringue. Beat together egg whites, cream of tartar, and 1/2 teaspoon vanilla extract in a medium mixing bowl. Mixture should form stiff peaks.

Combine shredded coconut with pie filling and spoon into the baked pie shell. Spread with meringue. Sprinkle coconut meal over meringue. Bake at 350 degrees in a preheated oven for 9 or 10 minutes until golden. Serve at room temperature or chilled. Refrigerate leftovers.

Variation: Milk can be increased to 3 cups. Omit the water.

Apricot Pineapple Pie

Yields a 9 inch pie

This luscious chilled fruit pie is easy to prepare.

- 1 baked 9 inch pie shell
- 1 can (16 ounce) sugarfree apricot halves OR 2 cups fresh apricot halves simmered in 1/2 cup water for 5 minutes
- 1 can (8 ounce) sugarfree crushed pineapple OR 1 1/2 cup fresh pineapple chunks simmered in 1/3 cup water for 5 minutes.
- 1/8 teaspoon salt
- 1/4 cup plus 1 teaspoon cornstarch or arrowroot powder
- 3/4 teaspoon Stevia Extract Powder
- 1/2 cup unsweetened applesauce
- 1 teaspoon vanilla extract, optional
- 1 recipe Whipped Cream (see index), optional

Drain apricot halves and reserve 1/2 cup juice. Pour remaining juice into a medium saucepan and cut apricots into small pieces. Add apricots, pineapple with its juice, and salt to saucepan. Bring to a boil. Dissolve cornstarch in reserved 1/2 cup juice and stir into heated fruit.

Reduce to simmer and cook, stirring, until mixture thickens.

Dissolve stevia in applesauce and add to filling. Stir in vanilla if used. Cool to room temperature, pour into crust, and chill until surface firms. Cover with plastic wrap and chill several hours. Top with Whipped Cream if desired.

Variation: Sprinkle toasted, unsulphured coconut over Whipped Cream.

Peanut Butter Pie

Yields a 9 inch pie

Peanut Butter at its finest!

- Pastry for a 1 crust shell, baked
- 1 teaspoon Stevia Extract Powder
- 1/2 cup water
- 2 tablespoons cornstarch or arrowroot powder
- 3 eggs, slightly beaten
- 3/4 cup milk
- 1 teaspoon vanilla extract
- 1/2 cup chunky natural peanut butter
- 1 cup whipping cream
- 1/4 teaspoon Stevia Extract Powder
- 1/4 teaspoon vanilla
- 2 tablespoons unsalted dry-roasted peanuts, crushed

Using a double boiler pan, dissolve 1 teaspoon stevia and cornstarch in water. Beat in eggs and milk. Place over boiling water and reduce heat to medium low. Cook, stirring until mixture thickens. Remove from heat and cool 10 minutes. Stir in 1 teaspoon vanilla and peanut butter. Cool to room temperature.

Beat together cream, 1/4 teaspoon stevia, and 1/4 teaspoon vanilla until soft peaks form. Do not over-beat. Fold into pie filling. Turn into the baked pie shell. Sprinkle crushed peanuts around the edges. Chill several hours.

Perfect Oat Crust

This crisp and flavorful crust is suitable for any pie.

- 2/3 cup rolled oats
- 2/3 cup barley flour OR whole wheat pastry flour
- 1/4 teaspoon salt
- 1/8 teaspoon Stevia Extract Powder
- 1/4 cup vegetable oil
- 1 1/2 tablespoons water

Use a blender to lightly chop oats. Combine with flour, salt, and stevia in an 8 inch pie dish. Add oil and water and stir with a fork to form a ball of dough. Cover and set aside 5 minutes so oats can soften.

Press dough evenly over sides and bottom of pie dish (if preferred, roll out between 2 waxed paper squares and place in pie dish). Prick with a fork in several places. Bake in a preheated oven at 350 degrees for 12 to 15 minutes or until lightly browned. Watch carefully. Cool on a rack.

This pie shell can also be filled and then baked according to a chosen recipe.

Tip: For a deep dish 10 inch pie crust use 1 cup rolled oats, 1 cup barley flour, 1/4 teaspoon salt, 1/4 teaspoon Stevia Extract Powder, 6 tablespoons vegetable oil, and 2 1/2 tablespoons water.

Easy Oil Pastry

Yields a 10 inch crust

Mix right in the pie dish.

- 1½ cups whole wheat pastry flour
- ⅛ teaspoon Stevia Extract Powder
- ¼ teaspoon salt
- ½ cup vegetable oil
- 2 tablespoons milk or water

In a 10 inch pie dish mix flour, stevia, and salt. Add oil and milk, then stir with a fork just until dough holds together.

Press evenly over sides and bottom of pie dish. Flute edges and prick pastry with a fork in several places. Bake in a preheated 360 degree oven for 10 to 12 minutes or until lightly browned.

This crust may also be baked after it is filled.

Variation: Reduce oil to ¼ cup and add ¼ cup applesauce. Bake crust 13 to 15 minutes.

Rolled Oil Pastry

Rolls out easily and bakes crispy.

- 2 cups whole wheat pastry flour
- 1/4 cup rice flour
- 1/4 teaspoon salt
- 1/8 teaspoon Stevia Extract Powder
- 2 teaspoons nonfat dry milk or soy beverage powder
- 1/2 cup vegetable oil
- 1/3 cup cold water

Stir first 5 ingredients in a medium mixing bowl. Pour measured oil and water together and add to dry ingredients. Lightly stir with a fork. Divide into 2 pieces and form into slightly flattened disks. Place each disk between 2 squares of waxed paper.

Slightly dampen counter to hold lower paper in place. Roll each disk of dough to an 11 inch circle. Fill according to recipe used. Roll out upper crust and use as directed in recipe.

Variation: Oat flour can replace the rice flour.

Barley Flour Crust

Yields a 9 or 10 inch crust

This whole grain crust is flaky and flavorful.

- 1 cup pus 2 tablespoons barley flour
- ¼ teaspoon salt
- ⅛ teaspoon Stevia Extract Powder
- 6 tablespoons butter
- 1 large egg
- 1 tablespoon water or more as needed

Stir or sift together flour, salt, and stevia. With a pastry blender cut in butter. Break egg into a cup. Add 1 tablespoon water and beat slightly with a fork. Add to the flour mixture and combine using the fork until a ball can be formed. Add more water if needed.

The pastry can be rolled out on a lightly floured surface or between 2 squares of waxed paper. Fit crust into pie dish and prick with fork in several places. Bake in a preheated oven at 360 degrees for about 10 or 12 minutes or until just lightly browned.

Crisp Cookie Crust

Oats and spice in a pie shell. Press into pie dish.

- 1/4 cup butter or non-hydrogenated soy margarine
- 1/2 cup whole wheat pastry flour
- 1/4 teaspoon Stevia Extract Powder OR ¾ teaspoon Green Stevia Powder
- 3/4 teaspoon cinnamon
- dash of nutmeg
- 3/4 cup rolled oats, lightly chopped in a blender
- 1/3 cup finely chopped walnuts
- 1 or 2 tablespoons natural apple juice

Melt butter* over very low heat in a 9 inch pie dish. In another pan, stir together flour, stevia, and spices. Mix in oats and walnuts. Stir into butter in pie dish. Sprinkle on apple juice and stir until mixture is clumpy. Press evenly and firmly over sides and bottom of pie dish. Prick the crust with a fork several places. Bake at 350 degrees in a preheated oven about 12 to 15 minutes or until lightly browned. Cool.

This crust can also be filled before baking.

Variations: For less salt, use unsalted butter.

*Tip: Do not melt margarine. It stirs in as is.

Chapter 14
Frosty Frozen Desserts

Here's a treasure trove of frozen dessert recipes you'll love to prepare and eat. They range from high to low in fat content. Have a party with Lemon Ice Cream on Grandma's Apple Pie. Pink Pear Sorbet, though low calories, is big on flavor. A few of the recipes are dairy free.

Freeze these desserts in your refrigerator's freezer section. The time required varies. No need to stand by the door watching, however. If the dessert freezes too hard, just soften at room temperature and beat again.

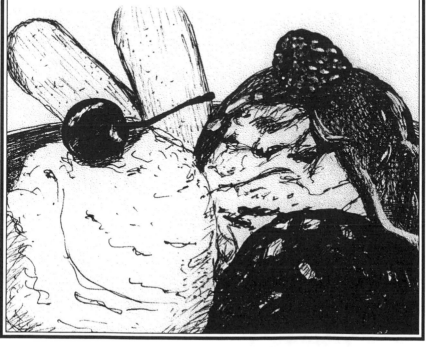

Lemon Ice Cream

Sweet cream with a lemon zing.

- 1/2 teaspoon Stevia Extract Powder OR 1 1/2 to 2 teaspoons Green Stevia Powder
- 1 cup milk, skim or whole
- 1 cup whipping cream
- 1/4 cup fresh lemon juice
- 1/8 teaspoon lemon extract

Combine stevia, milk, and cream in a small, deep mixing bowl. Stir to dissolve stevia. Cover with plastic wrap and freeze 1 or 2 hours until solid around the edges.

Remove from freezer. Add lemon juice and extract. Beat thoroughly and replace the plastic wrap. Return to freezer.

After 2 hours beat again. Freeze some more until consistency is firm but still soft enough to dip. This entire process requires about 6 hours and very little effort.

For leftovers, remove from freezer about 1/2 hour before serving to allow for softening. Whip again if desired.

Variations:

- The amount of stevia and lemon extract can be varied according to taste. Equal amounts of lemon extract and vanilla extract can be used.
- In place of dairy milk use soymilk.

Frozen Strawberry Cream   Yields 6 servings

This delicious strawberry-cream combo is a classic.

- 1 cup whipping cream
- 1 cup milk, skim or whole
- 1/2 teaspoon Stevia Extract Powder
- 1/4 teaspoon vanilla extract
- few drops of lemon extract
- 2 cups strawberries, fresh or frozen (thawed)
- 2 tablespoons fresh lemon juice

Combine cream, milk, stevia, vanilla, and lemon extracts in a medium mixing bowl. Stir to dissolve stevia. Cover with plastic wrap and place bowl in the freezer an hour or until frozen solid around the edges only. Remove from freezer.

Mash strawberries and add to the cream mixture. Add lemon juice and beat thoroughly. Re-cover with plastic wrap and freeze an additional 3 or 4 hours. Serve when partially frozen or, for a fluffier dessert, whip again immediately before serving.

Freeze leftovers. Remove from freezer an hour before serving. Freezer temperatures vary, which affects the total time required to prepare this dessert.

Variations:
- Use soymilk in place of dairy milk.
- Other fruits can replace strawberries.

Blueberry Soft Serve Yogurt   Yields about 1 quart

Enjoy the richness of ice cream with fewer calories.

- 1/2 cup natural apple juice
- 2 tablespoons agar agar or 1 envelope unflavored gelatin
- 1/4 cup natural apple juice
- 1 1/3 cups fresh or frozen blueberries
- 2 tablespoons rice beverage powder or nonfat dry milk
- 3/4 teaspoon Stevia Extract Powder
- 1 or 2 teaspoons fresh lemon juice
- 1/2 teaspoon vanilla extract
- 2 cups soy yogurt or plain yogurt

Place 1/2 cup apple juice and agar agar (or gelatin) in a small saucepan to soften. Bring juice and agar agar mixture to a boil, then simmer 5 minutes (or place juice with gelatin over low heat to dissolve). Remove from heat and keep at room temperature.

In a blender container, process 1/4 cup apple juice and remaining ingredients. With blender still running, slowly pour agar agar solution (or gelatin solution) into the center of the blender. Process thoroughly. Pour into a stainless steel bowl, cover, and freeze to "soft serve" consistency. This takes 3 to 5 hours.

For leftovers, Remove from freezer 45 minutes before serving and process in a blender to a smooth texture.

Variation: This recipe works well with strawberries also. Adjust the amount of stevia according to berry sweetness.

Pink Pear Sorbet Yields 4 servings

Enjoy this heavenly blend of fruit flavors. Easy, too!

- 1/2 teaspoon Stevia Extract Powder
- 2 tablespoons fresh lemon juice
- 2 medium pears
- 1/3 to 1/2 cup cherry juice (sugarfree frozen juice concentrate, diluted)

In a small mixing bowl, dissolve stevia in lemon juice. Peel, core, and chop pears. Stir into lemon mixture. Cover mixing bowl and freeze for 2 or 3 hours.

When ready to serve, place pears and 1/3 cup cherry juice in blender bowl. Process until smooth while adding remaining juice as needed for soft sorbet. Serve immediately. Freeze leftovers. Remove from freezer 30 to 45 minutes before serving.

Variations:
- Adjust the amount of stevia as needed.
- A cherry juice blend (with other fruit juices) also tastes fine in this dessert.

Maple Nut Ice Cream

Freeze bananas the day before for this "almost instant" treat.

- frozen banana chunks to equal 3 bananas
- 1/2 cup plus 2 tablespoons natural apple juice
- 1/16 teaspoon Green Stevia Powder
- 1/16 to 1/8 teaspoon natural maple flavoring
- 2 tablespoons unsweetened nutbutter, preferably raw, such as cashew or almond.

Place about 1/2 of a banana, the 1/2 cup juice, stevia, flavoring, and nutbutter in a blender bowl. Cover and process on medium setting until the mixture is almost smooth. Then turn on high and gradually add banana chunks, blending until smooth using all the banana. While adding bananas, the mixture will thicken, so add the remaining 2 tablespoons apple juice, plus more if needed, to make a soft ice cream consistency.

Serve immediately.

Variation: Unsweetened white grape juice can replace the apple juice for a slightly different flavor.

Soft Blackberry Sherbet

Yields 4 servings

This dairy free dessert is a real delight. Try other fruit as well!

- 3 fresh bananas
- 2¼ cups frozen sugarfree blackberries or fresh blackberries
- ¹⁄₁₆ teaspoon Stevia Extract Powder OR ¼ teaspoon Green Stevia Powder
- ¼ teaspoon vanilla extract
- 1 teaspoon fresh lemon juice

Process bananas briefly in blender bowl. Turn off power and add a few blackberries, stevia, vanilla extract, and lemon juice. Turn blender on low and gradually turn to full power. Add remaining blackberries a few at a time. When smooth pour into dessert dishes. Serve immediately.

Variations: Sliced peaches, strawberries, or blueberries may be substituted for blackberries.

Frozen Fruit Cup

Mixed fruit in a mellow yogurt base.

- You'll need 12 disposable 6 to 8 ounce cups
- 1 can (8 ounces) sugarfree crushed pineapple
- 1 ripe banana
- 3/4 cup low fat cottage cheese
- 4 tablespoons frozen unsweetened apple juice concentrate (do not dilute)
- 1/2 teaspoon Stevia Extract Powder
- 1 cup plain low fat yogurt or soy yogurt
- 1 tablespoon fresh lemon juice
- 1 teaspoon vanilla extract
- 1 1/2 cups fresh or frozen blueberries
- 3 fresh peaches, peeled and chopped
- Optional garnishes: fresh fruit pieces, mint leaves, shredded coconut

Drain pineapple and reserve juice. Set pineapple aside. Combine in a blender bowl the banana, cottage cheese, apple juice concentrate, stevia, yogurt, lemon juice, vanilla extract, and reserved pineapple juice. Process until smooth.

Place 6 plastic cups in each of 2 bread pans. Divide the pineapple, blueberries, and peaches evenly among the cups. Pour the blended base mixture over the fruit. Cover with a sheet of plastic wrap and freeze.

Thaw 1/2 to 1 hour before serving. Un-mold and garnish with fresh fruit pieces and mint leaves or coconut. Or simply serve in the cups.

Variations:
- 1 1/2 cups sliced fresh strawberries can be used in place of blueberries.
- Substitute 1/2 cup tofu for 1/2 cup of the yogurt.

Rhubarb Pineapple Freeze

Yields 12 servings

Cupcake size frozen yogurt and fruit desserts.

- 12 disposable 2½ x 1¼ inch paper baking cups
- 2 ripe bananas, mashed
- 1 cup lowfat yogurt or soy yogurt
- ½ teaspoon Stevia Extract Powder
- 1 cup Sweet Rhubarb Sauce (see index)
- 1 cup fresh cubed pineapple, including juice, or 1 (8 ounce) can crushed pineapple
- Blackberry Sauce (see index) as a topping, optional

Line muffin cups with the paper cups.

Mix bananas, yogurt, stevia, Rhubarb Sauce, and pineapple in a medium bowl. Spoon into paper cups. Freeze for 1½ to 3 hours. Remove paper cups and place desserts on plates. Garnish as desired. Blackberry Sauce makes an attractive, delicious topping.

Ginger Pineapple Sherbet

These delightful flavors blend well for a tangy frozen dessert.

- 1 1/2 cups fresh pineapple chunks or 1 1/2 cups cooked and drained pineapple spears
- 1 large banana
- 1/4 teaspoon Stevia Extract Powder OR 3/8 teaspoon Green Stevia Powder
- 1/2 teaspoon Ginger Tea Concentrate (see index) OR ginger powder to taste
- 1/2 cup plain yogurt OR soy yogurt
- 2 teaspoons fresh lime OR lemon juice

Place all ingredients in a food processor bowl or blender bowl and process until smooth. Pour into a stainless steel bowl, cover, and place in freezer. Stir once an hour and freeze 4 to 6 hours. Serve when it's the consistency you like.

Chapter 15

Other Tasty Treats

Delightful surprises await you in this chapter. Make your own salt-free seasoning blend, vegetable stock, or yogurt. Surprise your child Easter morning with miniature nests of tiny "eggs," really a carob and coconut confection. Enjoy shaping your own candy designs as well!

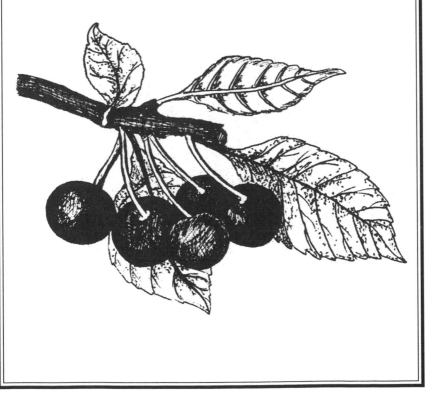

Homemade Yogurt with Fruit
Yields 1 quart yogurt

Enjoy the creamy tang of yogurt with stevia sweetened fruit.

- 3 3/4 cups water
- 1 1/4 cups nonfat dry milk
- 2 tablespoons plain yogurt with live yogurt culture (check labels) or use "yogurt starter*"
- fruit jam, spread, or sauce (see index) or fresh fruit
- Stevia Extract Powder as needed

Use a Yogurt Maker following manufacturer's instructions or use an electric skillet set on low. Experiment to determine where on the dial your skillet will maintain a temperature between 95 and 110 degrees. Use very clean utensils.

Whisk together water, dry milk, and yogurt. Pour into yogurt maker containers or 4 (8 ounce) jelly jars. Do not cover the jars as they cook but do cover the skillet. Do not disturb as yogurt thickens, 4 to 8 hours. Cool at room temperature. Cover jars and refrigerate. Serve with fruit jam or sauce, or fresh fruit sweetened to taste. Dissolve 1/8 to 1/4 teaspoon Stevia Extract Powder in 2 teaspoons water and stir with 1 cup prepared fruit.

Tip: The yogurt without fruit can be used in recipes calling for plain or unflavored yogurt.

* "Yogurt Starter" is available at health food stores.

Soy Yogurt

Yields 1 pint

Follow general directions for processing Homemade Yogurt with Fruit (see index). Use the following ingredients.

- 1 pint soymilk
- 1 tablespoon yogurt with active yogurt culture OR use "yogurt starter."

Whisk together soymilk and yogurt in a flat casserole which will fit into your electric skillet. Place in skillet and set temperature control. OR pour into yogurt maker containers. Do not disturb yogurt as it congeals, which requires 2 to 6 hours. Use the tip of a spoon to test the consistency of the yogurt.

Refrigerate. Use within 5 days. Be sure to save 1 tablespoon yogurt to start your next batch.

Variation: For vanilla yogurt, whisk in 1/8 teaspoon Stevia Extract Powder and 1/4 teaspoon vanilla extract with other ingredients.

Cottage Sour Cream

Yields 1 pint

Tastefully tops baked potatoes, vegetables, or desserts.

- 1¾ cups lowfat cottage cheese
- ½ cup plain yogurt OR soy yogurt
- ¹⁄₁₆ teaspoon Stevia Extract Powder
- 2 or 3 teaspoons fresh lemon juice

Measure cottage cheese into a mesh strainer set over a bowl. Drain 5 minutes. Drained liquid can be reserved for another use.

Place cheese, yogurt, stevia, and lemon juice in a blender bowl. Process to a smooth consistency. Refrigerate. Use within a few days.

Tip: For a thicker product, add some nonfat dry milk.

Wholegrain Crackers

Eat right from the oven for maximum crunch and flavor.

- 2 cups rolled oats
- 3/4 cup whole grain cornmeal
- 1/2 teaspoon salt
- 1/4 cup cornstarch OR arrowroot powder
- 2/3 cup water
- 1/8 teaspoon Stevia Extract Powder
- 1/3 cup vegetable oil

Stir together oats, cornmeal, salt, and cornstarch. Set aside.

In another bowl combine water, stevia, and oil. Stir in dry ingredients. Cover and allow to set 30 minutes.

Form walnut size balls and flatten to 2 ½ inch diameter crackers. Place on lightly oiled baking sheets. Bake in a preheated oven at 400 degrees for 12 or 13 minutes. Watch carefully – crackers should be golden brown. Serve hot with hot soup.

Tip: Crackers can be pressed thinner and cooked for a shorter time. They will be more crisp.

Variation: Stir in 1/2 teaspoon Garden Blend Seasoning (see index) or other herbs with dry ingredients.

Salmon Filling

Yields 2 cups

Use in sandwiches, on crackers, or as a tasty dip.

- 1 can (14¾ ounce) pink salmon
- ½ cup soft tofu
- 2 teaspoons fresh lemon juice
- ¼ teaspoon salt
- 1⁄16 teaspoon Stevia Extract Powder OR
  ¼ teaspoon Green Stevia Powder
- ½ teaspoon Garden Blend Seasoning (see index)
  or other herbs to taste.
- ½ teaspoon dry dill weed
- ¼ cup finely chopped celery
- 2 tablespoons minced parsley

Drain salmon and reserve 2 tablespoons broth. Flake salmon and mash bones with a fork.

In a small bowl beat together tofu, lemon juice, reserved salmon broth, salt, stevia, seasoning, and dill weed. Stir in salmon, celery, and parsley. Cover and refrigerate.

Variation: Use 4 ounces Neufchatel cheese in place of tofu. Omit salt.

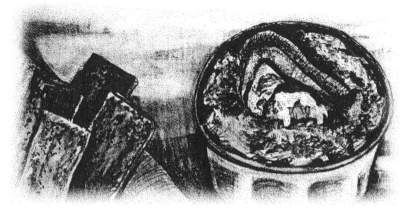

Egg Salad Sandwich Filling
Yields filling for 6 sandwiches

Great on whole grain bread with lettuce or spinach.

- 1/2 cup Basic Salad Dressing (see index)
- 2 tablespoons minced parsley
- 1/2 teaspoon onion powder OR minced fresh onion to taste
- 1 teaspoon Dijon-style mustard
- 1/4 teaspoon tarragon flakes
- 1/4 teaspoon salt, optional
- 1/4 teaspoon Green Stevia Powder OR 1/16 teaspoon Stevia Extract Powder
- 1/2 teaspon seasoned rice vinegar OR vinegar of your choice
- 4 hard boiled eggs, chopped

Combine all ingredients, except eggs, in a medium bowl. Stir in eggs. Cover bowl and refrigerate until meal preparation time.

Variations: Add 2 tablespoons grated dill pickle or chopped green pepper. A sprinkling of Garden Blend seasoning (see index) can also be added.

Savory Vegetable Stock
Yield varies with the amount of trimmings used

A vegetarian soup base for recipes requiring stock or broth.

- scrubbed vegetable trimmings (saved for up to 5 days)
- bay leaf and other herbs
- handful of parsley or spinach
- 2 potatoes, scrubbed and cubed
- 2 onions, coarsely chopped
- 4 summer squash, chopped
- 2 carrots, scrubbed and cubed
- 3 ribs celery with tops
- 2 cloves garlic, peeled
- 1 cup chopped green beans, stems removed
- 1/8 teaspoon Green Stevia Powder (minimum)
- Garden Blend Seasoning (see index)
- lite soy sauce (optional)

With paper towels pat trimmings dry, place in a plastic bag, and refrigerate. The trimmings can include parsley stems, turnip tops, bell pepper seeds and cores, pea pods, outer leaves of greens, etc. Leave the bag top open for some air and place in crisper drawer.

When ready to prepare the stock, rinse the trimmings well, place in soup pot, and add bay leaf and other herbs of your choice. Cover with water. Bring to a boil and then simmer 1 to 2 hours. Strain and reserve stock. Discard pulp.

While trimmings simmer, place remaining ingredients in a Dutch oven. Cover with water, bring to a boil, and then simmer until soft. Strain off broth. Reserve vegetables for later use.

Combine trimmings stock with that from the vegetables. Stir in 1/8 teaspoon Green Stevia Powder per quart of stock. Adjust seasonings.

Tip: Include only a few trimmings from the cabbage family as they are strongly flavored.

Garden Blend Seasoning   Yields about 3 tablespoons

A salt-free herbal mix for table use or cooking

- 1 teaspoon dry crushed basil leaves
- 3 teaspoons onion powder
- 1/4 teaspoon Green Stevia Powder
- 1/8 teaspoon pepper, optional
- 1 3/4 teaspoon garlic powder
- 1/2 teaspoon dry thyme leaves
- 1 teaspoon dry parsley leaves

Choose a container with a tight-fitting lid. Measure all ingredients into the container and shake to mix well.

Store in a dry, cool place. Stir or shake before using.

Tip: This green stevia blend will add flavor to salads, pasta, vegetables, or meats. Substitute some of your family's favorite herbs in the recipe, if desired.

Pesto Veggie Dip   Yields 1 cup dip

The piquant flavor of pesto combines well with the beans.

- 1 cup cooked Great Northern Beans
- 2 tablespoons Pesto Sauce (see index)
- 1/16 teaspoon Green Stevia powder OR a pinch of Stevia Extract Powder
- 2 tablespoons reserved bean broth or water

Drain cooled beans reserving cooking broth, if any remains. Place beans, Pesto Sauce, stevia, and 1 tablespoon broth or water in blender bowl. Process, pushing down the mixture with a rubber spatula as needed. ALWAYS SWITCH OFF THE MACHINE WHEN PUTTING A UTENSIL IN IT. Blend until almost smooth, using more of the liquid, if needed. Store, covered, in the refrigerator. Serve with raw vegetables, bread sticks, crackers, or chips.

Mini-Nest Confections

Fill the nests with tiny pastel jelly beans or peanuts.

- 1 cup sugarfree carob chips
- 1 tablespoon butter
- 1/8 teaspoon Stevia Extract Powder
- 1 cup unsulphured, shredded coconut (if shreds are quite large, chop briefly in a blender)
- small sugarfree jelly beans or large peanuts

Place chips and butter in a double boiler pan set over simmering water. When chips melt, stir to a smooth mass. Add coconut and mix to coat the shreds with carob.

Line a pan with waxed paper. Using 2 forks, work with about 2 tablespoons carob mixture at a time forming nest shapes on the waxed paper. Nests will be about 2 inches in diameter.

Cover and Chill. Add 3 jelly beans or peanuts to each nest and serve.

Tip: Double the recipe and make nests large enough to hold a scoop of frozen yogurt or sherbet. Serves 6.

Zesty Glazed Red Beets

Sweet beet slices in a citrus sauce

- 2 1/2 cups cooked beet slices (this requires about 3 large beets)
- 1 tablespoon cornstarch
- 1/3 cup beet juice reserved from cooking
- 1 teaspoon grated orange peel, orange part only
- juice from 1/2 an orange
- juice from 1/2 a small lemon
- 2 teaspoons cider vinegar
- 1/8 teaspoon Stevia Extract Powder
- 1 tablespoon butter

Dissolve cornstarch in the beet juice in a medium saucepan. Add the orange juice, lemon juice, vinegar, and stevia. Cook over medium heat until clear and bubbly, stirring well. Add the beets, orange rind, and butter. Heat through and serve.

Variation: This dish may also be served chilled. Omit butter. Refrigerate.

Chapter 16
South of the Border

The United States enjoys many styles of ethnic cooking. Here we feature several dishes popular in the Mexican tradition, which can now be deliciously sweetened with stevia.

If sweet and spicy is your choice, flip to Sweet Cinnamon Chips or Sweet Potato Pie. Jalapeno pepper is the "hot" ingredient in Heart Warminí Corn Muffins, which uses either yellow or blue whole grain corn meal.

This hearty cuisine is easy to prepare and features readily available ingredients.

Turkey Salsa Soup

Choose mild or "hot" salsa for this "soup with a zing."

- 1½ cups vegetable or turkey broth
- 1 cup cooked turkey cubes
- 1½ cups corn, fresh or frozen
- 1 cup tomato salsa
- ¼ cup chopped sweet red peppers
- 1 can (4 ounces) chopped green chilies, drained
- 2 tablespoons minced fresh parsley
- ⅛ teaspoon Green Stevia Powder
- Garden Blend Seasoning to taste (see index)

Measure all ingredients into a saucepan. Bring to a boil, then reduce to a simmer. Cook 15 minutes. Serve.

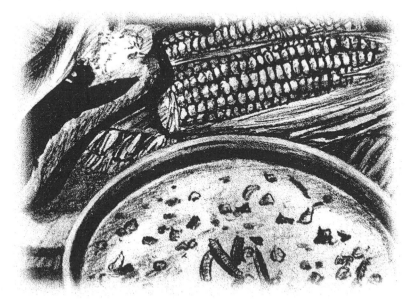

Fried Bananas

Delicate fruit flavors blend well for this easy dessert.

- 2 tablespoons cornstarch or arrowroot powder
- 1/2 teaspoon Stevia Extract Powder
- 2 cups natural white grape-peach juice combination
- 4 bananas
- 2 tablespoons butter
- Peach slices and fresh mint leaves for garnish, optional

Combine first 3 ingredients in a small saucepan. Bring to a boil and then simmer 1 minute to thicken. Set aside.

Melt butter in a large skillet. Split bananas lengthwise and then cut in half crosswise. Over medium heat gently cook bananas to a golden brown, turning once. This takes only 3 to 5 minutes.

Spoon sauce over bananas and continue cooking 1 minute. Ladle into dessert dishes and garnish as desired.

Variation: Omit grape-peach juice and use natural apple juice plus 1 teaspoon vanilla. Garnish with a dash of cinnamon.

Pear Bread Pudding

Yields 9 servings

Either 6 slices of homemade bread or 7 slices of bakery bread are used for this recipe.

- 3 1/2 cups toasted whole wheat or multi-grain bread squares
- 2 cups water
- 1 1/4 teaspoons cinnamon
- 1 1/2 teaspoons Stevia Extract Powder OR 4 teaspoons Green Stevia Powder
- 1 teaspoon vanilla extract
- 2 tablespoons butter
- 2/3 cup currants
- 1/2 cup chopped almonds or pecans
- 2 ripe pears
- 1/3 cup shredded mild cheese or brick style soy cheese

Toast bread and then cut into large squares.

In a large saucepan heat water to very hot. Remove from heat and stir in cinnamon, stevia, vanilla extract, butter, currants, and almonds. Gently fold in the toast.

Peel, core, and thinly slice the pears. Fold into the pudding mixture.

Lightly oil an 8 inch square baking dish. Spoon pudding into the dish, cover and bake in a preheated 350 degree oven for 30 minutes. Remove cover and top with cheese. Bake, uncovered, an additional 10 minutes. Serve warm. Refrigerate leftovers.

Date Empanadas

These individual fruit pies are baked rather than fried.

- 1 1/2 cups thick, natural applesauce
- 1 teaspoon cinnamon
- 1/4 teaspoon Stevia Extract Powder OR 1 teaspoon Green Stevia Powder
- 1 3/4 cups finely chopped dates
- 3 cups whole wheat pastry flour
- 1/2 teaspoon Stevia Extract Powder OR 1 teaspoon Green Stevia Powder
- 1/4 teaspoon salt
- 2 teaspoons baking powder
- 1/2 cup butter
- 2 eggs
- 1/2 cup plus 2 tablespoons water
- melted butter (about 1/4 cup)

Stir together applesauce, cinnamon, 1/4 teaspoon stevia, and dates for filling. Set aside while preparing dough.

Thoroughly mix flour, 1/2 teaspoon stevia, salt, and baking powder in a mixing bowl. Cut in butter until coarse crumbs form. Stir together eggs and water and add to flour mixture. Using a fork, stir to form a ball of dough. Cover with waxed paper and chill 1/2 hour.

Divide dough into 16 pieces. Roll pieces into 6 inch circles. Dampen edges with water and spoon on 3 tablespoons filling per piece. Fold dough over filling forming half circles. Press edges together with a fork and prick an opening in the top. Brush with melted butter.

Place empanadas on lightly oiled baking sheets and bake in a 350 degree preheated oven for 15 to 20 minutes. Cool on racks.

Mango Crème

Remember to freeze the bananas the night before.

- 2 bananas (frozen)
- 2 mangoes
- 2 tablespoons fresh lime juice or lemon juice
- 1/8 to 1/4 teaspoon Stevia Extract Powder
- 2 oranges, peeled and chopped, optional
- 2 kiwi fruit, peeled and sliced, optional

To prepare the bananas in advance, peel, break into halves, and drop in a plastic bag. Freeze.

Peel mangoes, remove seeds, and place the chunks of fruit in a blender bowl or food processor bowl. Add juice, stevia, and frozen bananas. Process until smooth. Pour into dessert dishes. Top with oranges or kiwi fruit, if used. Serve immediately.

Tip: This dessert may also be prepared by simply chilling the fruits before peeling and mashing all ingredients together.

Fruit Salad in Avocado Sauce   Yields 4 servings

Double the recipe for a fresh fruit luncheon.

- Lettuce leaves
- 2 bananas
- 2 kiwi fruit
- 2 cups fresh strawberries
- 1 large ripe avocado
- 2 tablespoons lime or lemon juice
- 1/4 teaspoon Stevia Extract Powder OR 3/4 teaspoon Green Stevia Powder
- 1 tablespoon chopped cilantro or parsley

Arrange lettuce leaves in a serving bowl or on a platter.

Thickly slice the bananas, kiwi fruit, and strawberries. Arrange atop the lettuce leaves.

Thoroughly mash together avocado, lime juice, and stevia using a fork. Spoon onto the salad and sprinkle with cilantro.

Serve immediately.

Variation: One mango or papaya, cubed, may be used in place of the kiwi fruit. Use a dash of ginger on each salad.

Corn and Pepper Relish

Yields 1 3/4 cups

A flavorful condiment to serve with poultry or vegetarian entrees.

- 1/4 teaspoon Stevia Extract Powder OR 3/4 teaspoon Green Stevia Powder
- 1 tablespoon dry minced onion
- 1/4 teaspoon celery seed
- 1/2 teaspoon dry mustard
- 1 tablespoon cider vinegar
- 2 tablespoons chopped jalapeno pepper
- 1/4 cup water
- 1 1/2 cups yellow corn, fresh or frozen
- 1/4 cup minced green sweet pepper
- 3 tablespoons fresh lime or lemon juice
- 2 tablespoons cooked pimento, chopped

Combine stevia, onion, celery seed, mustard, vinegar, jalapeno pepper, and water in a saucepan. Heat to a boil. Add corn and green pepper and simmer 9 or 10 minutes.

Remove from heat. Stir in lime juice and pimento. Spoon into a jar, cover, and chill overnight to blend flavors.

Heart Warmin' Corn Muffins   Yields 12 muffins

A moist, hearty bread with a jalapeno pepper 'kick'.

- 1 cup whole grain yellow cornmeal
- 1 cup whole wheat pastry flour
- 1/4 teaspoon Stevia Extract Powder OR 3/4 teaspoon Green Stevia Powder
- 2 teaspoons baking powder
- 1/4 teaspoons salt
- 2 eggs
- 1/2 cup natural applesauce
- 1/4 cup vegetable oil
- 3/4 cup shredded cheddar cheese or cheddar style soy cheese
- 2 tablespoons seeded, chopped jalapeno pepper
- 1 cup cream-style corn, fresh or canned

Oil the muffin cups.

Stir together the cornmeal, flour, stevia, baking powder, and salt. Use a large bowl to combine eggs, applesauce, and oil. Stir in dry ingredients and then add cheese, pepper, and corn. Stir just to combine. Divide batter among the muffin cups and bake in a preheated oven at 400 degrees for 15 to 17 minutes. Muffins should test done using a toothpick. Cool briefly, then remove from cups and serve.

Variations: Blue cornmeal can also be used in this recipe.

Tips: When using fresh corn, be sure to scrape the creamy part of the corn kernels from the cob. Also, wash hands after handling jalapeno pepper.

Sweet Cinnamon Chips

Yields 24 chips

Set out a bowl of applesauce for dipping!

- 3 whole grain 8 inch tortillas
- ½ teaspoon cornstarch or arrowroot powder
- ½ teaspoon cinnamon
- ⅛ teaspoon Stevia Extract Powder
- 1 dash allspice
- 1 tablespoon butter, melted

Preheat oven to 350 degrees.

Stir together cornstarch, cinnamon, stevia, and allspice. Brush tortillas with butter. Spoon spice mixture into a tea strainer and sift evenly over the tortillas. Cut tortillas into 8 wedges each and place on lightly oiled baking sheets. Bake 6 to 8 minutes or until lightly browned. Watch carefully to prevent burning.

Tip: Tortillas can be brushed with water in place of butter.

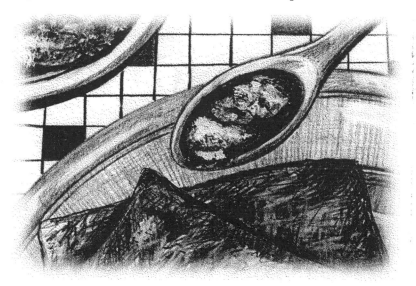

Old Fashioned Rice Pudding

Yields 8 servings

Mix this dessert right in the baking dish.

- 3/4 to 1 teaspoon Stevia Extract Powder
- 2 eggs, lightly beaten
- 1/4 teaspoon salt
- 2 cups milk or soymilk
- 1/3 cup raisins
- 2 teaspoons vanilla extract
- 1/4 teaspoon nutmeg
- 2 cups cooked brown rice

Preheat oven to 350 degrees.

Select a 2 quart casserole dish and mix together all ingredients except the rice. Lastly stir in rice.

Bake for 55 to 65 minutes or until firm. Serve chilled.

Tip: Pass a pitcher of milk to pour over the pudding

Sweet Potato Pie

Yields one 9 or 10 inch pie

This pie is pure perfection, but add some whipped cream if you like (see index).

- Pastry for a single-crust pie
- 3 medium size sweet potatoes, cooked
- 2 eggs, lightly beaten.
- 1 1/2 cups skim milk or soymilk
- 3 tablespoons butter, melted
- 1 teaspoon Stevia Extract Powder
- 1/2 teaspoon ginger
- 1/2 teaspoon cinnamon
- 1/4 teaspoon salt
- 1/4 teaspoon nutmeg
- 1 tablespoon fresh lemon juice
- few drops lemon extract

Preheat oven to 350 degrees.

Place prepared pastry in a pie dish and bake for 7 minutes only. Set aside.

Peel and mash potatoes and measure 2 cups pulp into mixing bowl. Stir in eggs, milk, and butter. Add remaining ingredients and mix thoroughly. Turn into the partially baked shell and bake 55 to 65 minutes. Filling should be just set near the center. If necessary, cover pie crust edges with foil during the last 15 minutes to prevent over-browning. Serve warm or chilled. Refrigerate leftovers.

Variation: Increase cinnamon to 1 teaspoon and replace lemon extract with 1 teaspoon vanilla extract.

189

Mexican Wedding 'Cakes'

Yields 40 'cakes'

These cookie-like confections are popular in several countries.

- 1 cup butter, softened
- 1 1/2 teaspoons vanilla extract
- 1/2 teaspoon Stevia Extract Powder
- 2 cups whole wheat pastry flour
- 1/2 cup finely chopped walnuts
- 1/4 teaspoon salt
- 1/2 recipe Powdered Stevia Garnish (see index)
- 1/16 teaspoon cinnamon, optional

Beat together the butter, vanilla extract, and stevia. Using a separate bowl, mix together flour, walnuts, and salt. Stir into the butter mixture using a heavy spoon. The dough will be stiff. Form into 1-inch balls and place on ungreased baking sheets. Bake in a preheated oven at 325 degrees for 20 minutes.

Cool in place on the baking sheets. Spoon Powdered Stevia Garnish into a shallow bowl and stir in cinnamon, if used. Carefully dip each cake into the garnish. Store in a covered container.

Index

195

Fluffy Vanilla Whip - 82
Oat Cinnamon Crunch - 83
Powdered Stevia garnish - 83
Whipped Cream - 81
Turkey Salsa Soup - 179
Vanilla Poached Pears - 119
Vanilla Yogurt Frosting - 114
Vegetarian Gelled Fruit Salad - 55
Very Orange Sauce - 70
Wheat Free Barley-Rye

Pancakes - 24
Whipped Cream - 81
Wholegrain Crackers - 171
Whole Wheat Burger Buns - 46
Whole Wheat Egg Noodles - 91
Yerba Mate Tea - 35
Yogurt
    Homemade with Fruit - 168
    Soy - 169
Zesty Glazed Red Beets - 177